*To Dede
Enjoy!
Blessings,
Betty Meabon
'08*

STEP BY STEP
A Collection of Poems of Inspiration and Travel

by Betty Meabon

Ambassador Press, LLC
in the spirit of excellence

Reynoldsburg, OH

Published by Ambassador Press, LLC
PO Box 722 Reynoldsburg, OH 43068
ambpress@insight.rr.com
www.ambassadorpressllc.com

Copyright © 2008 Betty Meabon

Cover Photo © 2008 Curtis Blake
www.curtisblakephotography.com

Cover Design © 2008 Imagine! Studios™
www.artsimagine.com

All rights reserved. No part of this publication may be reproduced or transmitted in any form or by any means, including informational storage and retrieval systems, without permission in writing from the copyright holder, except for brief quotations in a review.

ISBN 10: 0-9787850-5-3
ISBN 13: 978-0-9787850-5-5

Library of Congress Control Number: 2001012345

First Ambassador Press, LLC printing, November 2008

This book is dedicated to my family and to all those friends who offered words of encouragement about the way my poetry has inspired and touched their lives.

Thanks be to God for the Blessing of His Guidance and Inspiration to write.

Contents

Introduction 9

Step by Step 11

Seasons of Life 13
    Seasons of Life
    Spring
    My Secret Garden
    Summertime
    All Creatures Great and Small
    Unwanted Guests
    A Walk in the Woods
    A Peaceful Winter Day
    Snowmen
    Unbelievable Sights
    For Everything There Is a Season

The Glory of Christmas 29
    Christmas
    "The Glory of Christmas"
    What's Christmas All about Anyway?
    Advent Greetings
    Christmas Blessings
    Christmas Card Poetry
    Happy Holidays

Family 43
    My Family
    A Home That's Full
    That Special Family Cradle
    The Old Toy Trunk
    Family Traditions
    Those Kodak Moments
    A Woman of Faith
    Thoughts and Advice from Grandma
    My Creed
    My Life in Rhyme

Inspirational Thoughts and Blessings.................................. 63
    Blessings
    How Do You Spend Your Time?
    Surprises
    God Has a Plan
    It's All about Love
    Do You Believe in Angels?
    Life Is Fragile—Handle with Prayer
    Why Me, Oh, God, Why Me?
    When Life Gives You Lemons
    Choices
    Each New Day
    Fruit of the Spirit
    Spiritual Gifts
    Prayer
    Friendship
    Smile
    Music
    Don't Give up!

In Celebration of Central College Presbyterian Church 87
    The Church's One Foundation
    Step Out of the Boat!
    By One Spirit
    Christ Knocks at the Door
    God Is in Control
    Sacrifice
    Expect a Miracle
    Isn't It Interesting How the Lord Works?
    Trust in the Lord
    The Ellsworth Chapel Dedication
    The Dedication of the Pre-School Wing
    Tribute to "Rev" on His 35 Years as Pastor
    Tribute to Dr. Ellsworth's 40th Year
    "Building Our Faith" Groundbreaking
    Dr. Ellsworth's 45th Anniversary at CCPC
    Celebration of "Rev's" Service
    A Special Tribute to Our Pastor Ellsworth
    I'm Glad to Be at CCPC

Stewardship
  The Bakeless Bake Sale
  Prayer Shawl Blessing
  The Joy of Dolls
  Tell Me a Story
  Hats, Hats, Hats
  The CCPC Quilt
  A Challenge of Service
  Our Mission as Presbyterian Women

People and Places beyond the Familiar............................ 125
  Travels Introduction
  Countries Visited
  Enjoying the Journey
  Travel and Grow
  Egypt and the Nile
  Travels in the Holy Land
  Medical Mission to Honduras
  The Americas
  Adventures in Iceland and Greenland
  Adventures in Africa
  Rivers of Thought
  Travels in Europe
  Travels in India and Nepal
  Bucharest to Prague and So Much More
  Travels in the Far East
  Australia, New Zealand and the South Pacific
  Travel Souvenirs
  "Westward, Ho, the Wagons"
  Land of the Midnight Sun
  So Many Ways to Travel
  The Canadian Rockies
  Polar Bears and So Much More
  The Middle East
  People and Places beyond the Familiar
  Blessed to Be an American

About the Author 193

Endorsements 195

Introduction

Several friends have asked me many times
To publish a book with some of my rhymes.
I've often remarked that I can best say
The thoughts that inspire me in a rhyming way.

However, words don't always flow just right,
And it often takes lots of time to rewrite.
Compiling these poems took time, it's true,
But it's been fun to share these thoughts with you.

I hope some poems inspire you or give you a smile,
For that would make all my efforts worthwhile.
All glory, honor, and praise go to the Father above,
For He constantly guides me with His blessings and love.

My prayer is that you'll feel God touch your heart too,
As you read some of the writing that He inspired me to do.
So with that, I will close and let you begin,
To read some of the poetry that you'll find within.

Blessings,
Betty Meabon

Step by Step

Life is a journey of one step at a time.
Sometimes with mountains that seem hard to climb,
But when reaching the top…Oh, what a view!
And going back down is easier then too.

Sometimes we may think that the mountain's too high
And not worth the time and trouble to try.
Sometimes we may run up that mountain so fast
That we miss some pleasures as we pass.

Lord, help us to learn to enjoy each day
As step by step, we go on our way.

Seasons of Life

Seasons of Life

My favorite time of year is spring…
To see the blooms and hear birds sing.
The sun shines longer every day,
And then, soon summer's on its way.

And after summer comes the fall.
Some think this time is best of all…
The brilliant color of the leaves
Is certainly a sight to please.

Then after autumn, cold winds blow,
And here again, it's time for snow!
How could it be…it's gone so fast,
You turn around….the season's past.

And in our lives, that's also true,
For there, the time goes quickly too.
Some times in life, we wish could stay;
Just like a season's perfect day.

But then, there are days not so great,
And when they pass, we celebrate.
So overall, it's best to say,
"I'll make the most of every day!"

Spring

What a beautiful time of year...
When days grow longer and Spring is here!
Spring flowers bloom in colors bright,
And all the birds sing with delight.

The snow has finally gone once more.
Now flowers carpet the forest floor.
The trillium bloom in shades of white,
And bluebells are a glorious sight.

Spring beauties and violets are also seen;
Trout lilies grow by a little stream.
Trees are filled with blossoms white
And shades of pink, both dark and light.

How nice to smell the sweet, fresh air,
And notice new life everywhere.
Children go outside to play
And all enjoy a nice warm day.

For now that winter days have passed,
The skies are blue, not grey, at last.
I do think we enjoy spring more
Because the winter comes before.

For if all our days were perfect days,
We might forget to stop and praise
The Lord for all those special things...
Like the beauty that each springtime brings.

My Secret Garden

It's really not secret, but more like a retreat…
My yard is a garden, not like most on the street.
In the back, a fountain splashes into a pool,
Among many tall trees…on hot days, that's cool.

There's lots of lush ivy climbing over the ground.
It stays green all winter and reduces weeding, I've found.
Bulbs, perennials and native wildflowers also grow here,
And the birds plant more interesting new things each year.

All sorts of critters enjoy this garden as well.
Squirrels, rabbits, and raccoons all come here to dwell.
The birds and the butterflies seem happy here too,
And that's added pleasure, when they come into view.

There's not much need for mulching or raking of leaves;
Most care is now what a natural woodland receives.
Oh, yes, in the beginning it took much more care,
Like pulling some weeds that shouldn't grow there.

Some pruning's still needed, as everything grows,
For a garden always changes, as every gardener knows,
But a garden should not be "all work and no play."
It should be a place to retreat and enjoy every day.

Summertime

When summer arrives and the warm winds blow
And the pace of life goes from fast to slow,
When school is out and there's no homework to do,
There's more time for trips to the pool or the zoo.

There's time to go places with new things to see
Or perhaps a reunion with extended family.
Picnics and "Cook-outs" and "Sleep-overs" too…
All kinds of sports to go see or to do.

A day at the Fair is good family fun,
To see all sorts of things that people have done:
Crops they have raised, crafts they have made,
Animals and rides and even parades.

Evenings are longer for a walk in the park
Or maybe to catch fireflies after it's dark.
On some days, just to sit in the cool of the shade,
And maybe daydream while you sip lemonade.

Even the landscape changes now too.
Flowers and trees have a different hue.
Newborn animals start coming out
To experience what their new world's about.

Concerts outside in the fresh evening air;
Bicycle rides with the wind in your hair;
Neighbors come out to just have a chat…
Yard work, of course, encourages that.

In late summer, we begin to anticipate fall:
Back to school, meetings, schedules and all,
But a break in the routine was really sublime.
Isn't it great that we have summertime!

All Creatures Great and Small

This morning as I walked the trail,
I saw a deer with flashing tail;
And on that path, just yesterday,
A tiny rabbit nibbled hay.
It's fun to see them as I walk
Through Inniswood Nature Park.

Sometimes my backyard's like a zoo.
There I watch the chipmunks too,
And birds at feeders fly about,
While squirrels on limbs may just "hang-out."
The frogs and toads just sit and stare
As if they wonder why I'm there.

Sometimes raccoons get just too clever
With garbage cans and whatever.
The butterflies and hummingbirds
Are just too beautiful for words!
Yes, God has really blessed us all
With many creatures great and small.

Unwanted Guests

It was in the darkness of the night,
And I was fast asleep in bed
When I heard a noise, like scratching,
At the window by my head.
As I arose and took a peak
Out my window, on the roof,
I knew I wasn't dreaming,
For I now could see the proof.

There was a face…and with a mask…
Looking back at me.
Then as I stared a little longer,
In that darkness, I could see
That it was not just one face,
No…really, there were three!

Up on my roof and in the night,
The fear could have been great,
But I had seen this face before…
Just really not of late.

Now I knew what I was seeing,
Underneath that Harvest Moon….
A family, looking for a home,
For winter would be coming soon.
And I do often share my home
With guests that I invite…
Just not with these three young raccoons
In the middle of the night.

A Walk in the Woods

To walk in the woods, is my delight…
Among trees and all nature…what a beautiful sight!
Just to see the wild flowers and hear the birds sing,
Is such a relaxing and rewarding thing!

So often today we're in such a hurry,
So many are stressed with problems and worry.
Many things that stress us, can soon disappear.
With a walk in the woods, our minds get clear.

If we don't focus on problems, but on our blessings instead,
And on the things we enjoy, not all that we dread,
It's amazing how often those problems are solved.
With God's help and a clear mind the solutions evolve.

Of course, the work is still there that needs to be done,
But with a new outlook…sometimes it's more fun.
Communing with nature also gives one time to pray…
Yes, a walk in the woods can really "make your day."

A Peaceful Winter Day

Some folks think it's very strange
When you say you like the snow.
"How could you like it to be cold
And hear that north wind blow?"
"And then you need to shovel,
And how can that be fun?"
"And often in the winter
You barely see the sun!"

But there's something very peaceful
When the flakes float softly down,
For then almost like magic,
There's a blanket on the ground.
All the trees that once were bare
Now hold a touch of white
And when the moon shines on the snow
It sparkles in the light.

Sometimes it is a snow that packs,
And snowmen will be made,
Or snow forts for a battle
Or other games are played.
Sleds come out and ice skates too,
And snow angels might appear.
There really is a lot to like
In this wintry time of year.

Oh, yes, you have to bundle up
And find the gloves and hat;
Even dig the sweaters out
And turn up the thermostat,
But then just build a cozy fire
Or brew a cup of tea;
Pull out your very favorite book…
See how peaceful it can be.

It all depends on your outlook,
For that's what life's about.
You can either make the most of it
Or let it wear you out.
And life's too short not to enjoy
Every day and each new thing.
Besides, before you know it,
The winter will bring spring.

Snowmen

Snowmen aren't assembled
When they fall down from the sky;
But if the temperature is right,
And flakes aren't too wet or dry;
Then if that snow is packed together,
And it's formed into a ball;
With some imagination,
In not much time at all…
You can make a snowman,
And in your lawn he will remain,
Until the temperature warms up,
Or those flakes turn into rain.

That reminds me of our lives…
How quickly things can change.
We often think we're in control,
And our life is all arranged,
But really life's as fragile,
As the snowman, I must say,
And that should then remind us,
To make the most of every day…
And to live life to the fullest,
Yes, each day is such a gift;
Enjoy each minute's blessing,
For its passage can be swift!

And sometimes, like the snowman,
When things may look the best…
In an instant, things can turn around,
And put us to the test;
But unlike that snowman,
We don't need to melt away,
For with God's help and comfort,
We can face another day.

So tell your family that you love them,
Show your friends how much you care.
Take the time to "smell the roses;"
Look for beauty everywhere,
For you can be as happy
As you really choose to be.
You can look for negatives
Or the positive in what you see,
And like the snowman that was formed,
God has a plan for our lives too;
But you can choose to follow it,
Or not…it's all up to you.

Unbelievable Sights

Our world is filled with such unbelievable sights,
From deep in the sea to the mountainous heights;
Sunsets so beautiful and oceans so blue,
Birds and flowers of every hue.

There are all sorts of things, down deep in the sea:
Corals and sea creatures as bazaar as can be,
Fish by the millions with colors galore…
Beautiful sights, not seen from the shore.

Views from mountain tops, over lush valleys below,
No matter the season, always provide quite a show.
In full color, fall leaves are like a painting to see
Or the fresh fallen snow on an evergreen tree.

Waterfalls with rainbows and tropical trees,
Where butterflies, so fragile, often float in the breeze.
Yes, the beauty in God's creatures is unique too;
All sizes and shapes, in every pattern and hue.

What a wonderful world and what a delight,
That it's filled with all these beautiful sights.
This awesome creation our Lord has given
Must be the prelude to our home in heaven.

For Everything There Is a Season

"For everything there is a season," so often we've been told,
And that is just as true today, as it was in days of old.
For God has planned our very lives, although we may forget
That long before our lives began, His plan for us was set.

The Bible tells us that there is a "time for everything…"
And there are 'Seasons' in our lives, we know not what they'll bring.
There is a time to weep and laugh, a time for war and peace,
A time to mourn, a time to dance, a time to keep, and to release,

A time to build and to tear down, a time to gain and lose,
A time to love, a time to hate…most times we do not choose.
Some times are not what we would like, and we often wonder "why"…
Why did God choose this time to heal or perhaps for one to die.

Today, sometimes we are so stressed; time seems to fly so fast.
It's true that things move much faster now than they did in the past,
But we still get the same amount of hours in each day.
It's how we spend those hours that can often change our way.

If all our times were happy ones, how would we learn to cope?
When times were bad or really sad, perhaps we'd give up hope,
But God has given us a mind, so we can then decide,
To waste our time with worry or in His faithful love abide.

For there's one thing we can be sure of, our future's in His hand.
We may not know that future, but we know He has it planned.
And often when we have a chance to take a backward gaze,
Those times we thought were all so bad have helped in other ways.

They may have helped us to be strong when we'd otherwise be weak,
Or maybe opened up a door that we forgot to seek.
Yes, it is true, that God, indeed, does have our future planned;
And when a door is closed to us, a window's close at hand.

"For everything there is a season" and though we like some best,
When we really look at all of them, we know we have been blessed.

The Glory of Christmas

Christmas

My prayer for us all in this Holy Season
Is that we not forget that Christ is the reason,
And not only now, as we celebrate and give,
But throughout the year, in the way that we live.

May the Lord richly bless you with Peace, Joy, and Love,
And surround you with angels sent from above.
May you have health and happiness in the New Year,
And may your Holidays be filled with lots of Good Cheer!

"The Glory of Christmas"

This poem was written to tell the story
Of our trip to California, to see "The Glory."
We were 28 Christians, seeking to find
A Christmas experience of a different kind.
Right from the start, there was a challenging test,
But we all boarded the plane and traveled west.

The Capistrano Mission was quite a sight.
The Ranch and Renewal Center, another delight.
Oh, how we laughed and laughed some more…
Sometimes we laughed 'till our bellies were sore.
We studied and prayed too, along the way;
Searching the Scriptures for what God had to say.

A side trip to Lake Arrowhead, a beautiful sight
'Till the fog rolled over the mountain that night.
The Church Service on Sunday was also unique--
A spiritual experience asking, "What do you seek?"
'O Holy Night' with Gladys Knight singing,
The organ, the choirs…the whole church was ringing!

But "The Glory of Christmas" was, indeed, the highlight,
From the first trumpet sounding 'till they went out of sight.
The music, the angels (Wow! how they could fly])
The actors, the animals, that scenery, the sky--
It was Wondrous! Heavenly!...what more can I say?
The true meaning of Christmas came alive that day.

Yes, the trip was awesome and the fellowship the best.
How we witness and share this will be our next test.
Will we live every day to the fullest for Him?
Will we strive to do better and try not to sin?
If we really live daily as He taught us we should,
Then each day could be "Christmas," if only we would.

What's Christmas All about Anyway?*

At this time of year, as we pause and reflect—
We remember past times and with friends we connect.
This is also the Season when the New Year looms bright,
When resolutions are made to change wrong into right.
September 11 caused us to think even more
About what's really important and what might be in store,
About those we love and the values we cherish,
About democracy and freedom that we must not let perish.

To some, it might seem with this confusion and fear
That we should not even celebrate Christmas this year,
But that would just add to the stress and the strife
And give terrorists their goal, to change our way of life.
9-11, of course, may have filled us with fear--
How could it not, with an act so severe!
But what they forgot and what we need to make clear,
Is our faith and our courage and that we will persevere!

So what is Christmas all about anyway?
It's about Christ's Birth in that manger of hay;
It's about God's Gift to the world, that He loved so much;
It's about showing that love in the lives that we touch;
It's about caring and sharing and helping others;
It's about peace and goodwill and living like brothers.
It's about faith and hope and loving each new day;
It's about thanks for the blessings that God sends our way.
It's about joy and singing and keeping in touch
With all those we hold dear and love so much.
It's about worship and carols and gift-giving too
And memories that are cherished all the year through.

So, indeed, we need to have Christmas this year
And pray God will bless and remove the fear.
We pray for our country and those answering 'the call'
To protect our freedom and bring peace to us all.
May God give us wisdom and strength for each day
And keep us from evil along the way.
May your Christmas be all this and then even more,
And may the New Year have many blessings in store.

This holiday poem was written for Christmas following September 11, 2001

Advent Greetings

It's already here…where does the time go?
Yesterday it was summer, and now here's the snow!
The "hustle and bustle" has already begun,
And children keep asking, "How soon will it come?"
The shopping's in progress and it's time to send cards
To dear friends and family, to give our "regards."
Then there's the food and what shall we bake?
We look at the budget and wonder what gifts can we make.
There are concerts and plays…decorating and such,
The time seems so short and the activity so much!
But there's a spirit of love, of giving, and good cheer;
How nice it would be if that lasted all year!
How often, in this Season, do we stop and reflect
On all the Blessings we have…or is that what we neglect?
And does all the activity get in the way
Of the true meaning of Christmas…the Christ Child's Birthday?
Do we remember to give thanks to our Lord up above,
For our family and friends and all those that we love?
Do we help those in need…the sick, old, and poor,
Or is Santa first place and that trip to the store?
What would Christ do, I wonder, if He had to decide
How would He celebrate Christmas?…Should that be our guide?
He'd probably enjoy all the beautiful sights…
The music, gift giving…the twinkle of lights,
But He'd still stay focused on His Father above…
He'd spread PEACE and GOODWILL..HOPE, JOY, and LOVE.
He'd share and care for all men, like brothers…
He'd laugh and have fun but still think of others.
He'd praise God and thank Him for all that He's given;
He'd sing, pray and rejoice with the Angels in Heaven.
Wouldn't this world be better, if we'd all spread GOOD CHEER,
PEACE, GOODWILL, and LOVE every day of the year?
May your Christmas be blessed and your New Year too
With GOOD HEALTH and true JOY in all that you do!

Christmas Blessings

The snow is falling…lights glow all around…
Christmas music is playing…what a beautiful sound.
Yes, it's a special feeling that this season brings,
With greetings to send and carols to sing.
Hearts fill with JOY, LOVE, GOODWILL, and PEACE,
And there's HOPE that these blessings will never cease.

We praise God for the Christ Child, for it is His Birthday…
Long ago in that stable on a bed made of hay.
It's a glorious story that we hear every year…
How the angels told shepherds on a night so clear,
And the Wise Men followed with gifts to bring
To the babe in the manger, the Christ, our King.

It's a time to remember loved ones far and near
And thank God for our friends and family so dear.
It's a time to reflect on the year that has passed
And look forward to that New Year that seems to come fast.
So BEST WISHES & SPECIAL BLESSINGS are sent to you
Throughout this season and in the New Year too.

God's eternal love and blessings,
Like a fountain, has no end.
And the more we share with others,
The more that He will send.

As we celebrate this season
Of the Holy Christ Child's Birth,
Let us always keep this Spirit
Of good will and peace on earth.

May the marvelous love that came
That glorious Christmas night,
Continue to flow through your heart
And spread its wondrous light.

May good health, hope, joy and peace
Be with you and those most dear,
Not only at this blessed time
But each day throughout the year.

"But whoever drinks the water I give him will never thirst. Indeed, the water I give him will become a spring of water welling up to eternal life."
John 4:14

Original artwork by Rev. David Redding
The McCune Memorial Fountain

"Glory to God in the highest, and on earth peace, good will toward men."
Luke 2:14

The Flag, the Church, the Steeple
And the peaceful winter day,
Bring thoughts of many Blessings
As Christmas comes your way.

May Peace and Hope and Freedom
Fill both your heart and mind,
And the Love and Joy Christ taught us
Be shared with all mankind.

"Glory to God in the highest, and on earth peace,
good will toward men."
Luke 2:14

Please look closely at this picture,
It's a Christmas wish for you.
May it bring you lasting Peace and Joy,
Not just now, but all year through.

May the beauty of the flowers
Remind you of God's Love.
And may the Bible on the Table
Give you guidance from Above.

May the light seen in the candles
Shine through your life each day.
And the Cross be your Salvation
As you travel life's highway.

May the organ pipes inspire you
With glorious songs to sing,
To show your praise and Honor
To our Lord and Heavenly King.

The historic Ellsworth Chapel
Reminds us all once more,
Of our precious Christian heritage
And those who came before.

This Christmas wish is being sent
To family far and near,
To old friends and to new as well,
All those we hold most dear.

We wish you health and happiness
And blessings from above.
That peace and joy surround you
And fill your home with love.

"Glory to God in the highest, and on earth peace, good will toward men."
Luke 2:14

Happy Holidays

It's the Christmas Season and time for snow;
The stockings are hung and the lights are aglow.
Christmas music fills the air
And decorations are everywhere.

The children are glad that it's here at last,
But for some of us--it comes too fast.
We have cards and letters we want to send
To keep in touch with that special friend.

There are presents to wrap, cookies to bake,
The tree to trim and deadlines to make.
Sometimes we get so caught up in this
That the true Christmas meaning is one we miss.

For this is the birthday of our Dear Lord,
When the angels sang in one accord,
"Peace on earth, goodwill to all"—
It's a story, I'm sure, that you recall.

So may you have that PEACE and LOVE
And be truly BLESSED by the Lord above
With GOOD HEALTH and HAPPINESS all year through.
MERRY CHRISTMAS and HAPPY NEW YEAR too.

FAMILY

From this...

My Family

F....Fun, Friendly, and Fabulous...these words fit fine.

A....Attractive, Awesome, even Agreeable, most all the time.

M....Magnificent, Motivating, and Multiplying...how true!

I....Intelligent, Industrious, and Interesting in all they do.

L....Likeable, Loving, and Loyal...what more can I say?

Y....Yes, I'm blessed with a GREAT FAMILY, in every way.

...To this!

A Home That's Full

I may not clean closets the way that I should,
And sometimes you can write in the dust on the wood,
But my home is a happy one...or at least I hope so,
And in it, the memories and love overflow.

It's filled with needlework and paintings I've done,
And photos of family and projects begun.
There's music heard often as I teach and play,
And my gardens may even provide a bouquet.

Some may say that I have far too many things,
But what happy memories these treasures bring...
Like the little mementoes from travels I've had,
Photo albums of family...all these make me glad.

I often take time for a walk in the woods,
I'd rather do that than some things that I should.
But all things essential do seem to get done,
For life is too short not to have some fun!

I realize when I sit on my deck 'neath the trees,
How fortunate...I can do these things that please...
Of course, there are times when work gets in the way,
And that often happens, even on my best day.

But then, I thank God that I am able to do
The work that needs to be done and do fun things too.
That He's given me talents and a life that's been blessed.
Forgive me, Lord, if I've failed the "clean closet" test.

That Special Family Cradle

Built in the 1800s, of a plain design, in pine,
Is this old family cradle, made by a great-great grandfather of mine.
In it were rocked his children, and many more, by total count,
It's now held six generations...so that's really a large amount.
In '73 I restored it , and then painted a design,
For I felt that it was deserving, after all the lapse of time;
Also it had been in the flood that we had in '72,
So it really was in need, of an overall "re-do."
It's been passed down through the ages, to the oldest daughters in the clan;
That's how I came to have it, through the process of this plan.
For my Grandmother was the oldest daughter, as was her mother too,
Then to my Mother, who was oldest, and on to me...as tradition grew.
The photo is of my grandmother, when she came to visit me,
After the cradle's restoration in 1973.

The Old Toy Trunk

In the corner of our family room is where the old trunk sits.
When grandkids look for toys, that's the attention it now gets.
It once was bright and shiny, many generations ago,
And then spent time in attics, just holding "overflow."
It needed much attention when it came into my care;
But I felt it very worthy because of memories it would share.
It now has held old toys for 30 years or more,
Which is really quite a contrast from what it held before.
Perhaps it has held things that some would really treasure,
And now when opened, little ones just find fun and pleasure.
Don't you often wonder what stories we would know,
If this old trunk could tell of all that happened years ago?
For it's been a "family member" for many generations
And must have seen lots of change and even celebrations.
Yes, I really treasure antiques, for most have quite a legacy
Of cherished family memories, filled with love and history.

Family Traditions

When I think about the Holidays,
I'm reminded of how many ways
We celebrate…the same each year
With traditions that we all hold dear.
At Christmas, carols and the tree;
The Christmas lights we go to see;
The Church Service on Christmas eve;
The cards from loved ones we receive;
The stockings that we hang with care;
The decorations everywhere;
Special cookies that we bake---
Such fun to eat and decorate
With icing tinted green and red;
And houses made from gingerbread.
The gifts we give; gifts we receive;
Excited children who still believe,
But not just at Christmas is this true;
There are other celebrations too.
At Easter there are eggs to find…
Excitement of a different kind.
Thanksgiving and the same menu
For that becomes tradition too.
And other special times as well
Make stories that we later tell
Of love we shared; the laughs, the fun;
Good memories for everyone.
I'm sure you have traditions too;
If not…then why not start a few.

Those Kodak Moments

I really like to take pictures, as most everyone knows,
And my collection of albums just grows and grows.
I have many photos on my walls as well....
There's so much history that those pictures tell.

History of family and our fun times together,
In summer or winter...in all kinds of weather;
Birthdays and holidays of every kind,
Just a glance brings lots of memories to mind.

How much we've aged and how young ones have grown;
Places we've traveled and people we've known;
Sights that we've seen and things that we've done...
Most all remind me of times that were fun.

I seldom go places without camera in hand,
And often take pictures that weren't even planned
'Cause I never know when that "Kodak Moment" may be,
For the chance to capture another memory.

It really doesn't matter if the pose is just right.
It's just fun to remember the event or the sight.
Memories are precious, for life flies by so fast,
And the photos add history of life in the past.

So cherish today and all that it holds in store.
Be excited for the future and what's new to explore;
Take advantage of every "Kodak Moment" you see,
For someday those photos will show your history.

A "Woman of Faith"

"Faith," as defined by Webster, means trust,
And a belief in God, of course, is a must.
A "Woman of Faith" what then would that be?
It would mean many things, I think you'll agree.

Being a blessing to others, as we have been blessed,
Giving God the glory and always doing our best;
Being loving and caring, kindhearted and true;
Humble and patient, loyal and trustworthy too.

It means studying and sharing the Word of our Lord,
And helping others to see how great is His Reward.
It's peace and contentment and the glow of God's Love;
It's joy and fulfillment that come from Above.

A trip to the hospital to visit a friend;
A phone call to encourage or a note to send.
Living life to the fullest, as He showed us to,
And asking ourselves, "What would Jesus do?".

It's to pray without ceasing; to forget and forgive;
To be an inspiration to others by the way that we live.

Thoughts and Advice from Grandma

"The following poem was written at the request of a grandchild for a school project. Perhaps it summarizes some the advice and memories that you too may have shared with a loved one."

When you ask me to write of my memories of you
And give some advice, this was easy to do;
For I have many memories, and they are all good…
Isn't that just like a grandmother should?

Most of the time, we were lucky to live close-by,
So I remember the young days…all those questions of "Why."
I remember vacations to Grand Canyon and such,
When, at age five, you liked "Super Heroes" so much
That we feared you would try to fly over the rim,
'Cause Superman could do it, and you'd be like him.

There were fun times on holidays when the family was here,
And all the relatives gathered from far and near.
I can remember much more, but too long this would be,
And besides, I'd soon run out of poetry.

Now, for the advice…sometimes that's hard to hear,
But I'll make it quite simple and I hope very clear.
Let your actions and life always be an example,
For you've had good guidance and your talents are ample.

Use the mind that God gave you, for there's much you can do.
Be kind and generous, honest and true.
Be persistent and diligent to do what is right.
And pursue your dreams with all of your might.
Just remember that no matter what it is that you do,
You always have family that support and love you.

Prayers and blessings,
Grandma

My Creed

One day, I decided to write my "Creed,"
To collect my thoughts and then proceed.
For, as a Christian, that should be easy to do
To write about what I know to be true....
That God's the Father, Christ's His Son,
With the Holy Spirit, all three are one.

And as I wrote, the message flowed,
Of what He's given and what I owed.
I, then remembered, and it's so true,
How He said, "Ask and it will be given you."
He gives me guidance for each new day,
For how to live and what to say.

God gives me joy and peace of mind;
He gives me freedom of a special kind.
He gives me love and strength and cheer.
He gives me courage and takes all fear.
He gives me hope for the days ahead.
He gives me rest when I go to bed.

God's given me family and caring friends.
The more I have, the more He sends!
He gives me challenges all the time,
New things to conquer...new mountains to climb.
Sometimes I wonder, just what I'm to do,
Then he always responds with a message or two.

Now what can I give, I thought, to repay
For all these Blessings He gives me each day.
I can give of myself...my time, talent, and treasure;
But even that returns more than I can measure!
So as hard as I try to out-give Him, you see,
It always ends up that He gives more to me.

But now back to "My Creed," just what will it be?
I believe in forgiveness and life eternally;
I believe in The Father, loving and true,
And the list could continue, as I'm sure yours could too.
But how we respond to His love is the test,
What we do with His Blessings...do we give Him our best?

No, a "Creed" doesn't mean much, if we don't carry through.
Do you give to the Lord, as He's given to you?

My Life in Rhyme

Did you ever try to write the story of your life…
About all the things that happen…the good times and the strife?
Well, as I pondered this one day while sitting in the sun,
It seemed to be a challenge and so I have begun.

How does one tell a tale in rhyme of a life of all these years
And mention all the joyous times and also times of tears?
It isn't possible, of course, to tell it all, you see,
But I'll try to hit the highlights and not too boring be.

It all began with farm life, and I treasure that a lot;
Then a one-room school for the early education that I got.
And it was in those years that I learned so many things
About this world and all the joy that a loving family brings.

Parents, Aunts and Uncles, Grandparents, Brothers, too,
All played a most important part in my early life, it's true.
I learned of God and Nature and how farmers spend their days,
That nothing is impossible and hard work always pays.

Then off I went to High School, and these years have lots to tell.
I played piano, as before…now other instruments as well,
The band and choir and yearbook all provided extra fun,
And being Valedictorian…a special honor that I won.

Then to Indiana College, to start my Nursing School Career,
And back to Oil City and State Board time was here.
After graduation…a great marriage in 1954;
I still worked in nursing then but different than before.

Then the birth of our four children over the next 11 years,
And all the things a Mother does, plus many days as "Volunteer."
And through those years, of course, there were so many other things
That a fun and active family life always seems to bring.

We moved from Grove City to Butler, then on to Ohio;
When Roge's job required it…we always had to go.
Sometimes it wasn't easy to leave good friends behind,
But it did make us grow stronger, and new friends we'd always find.

We traveled lots of places and camped and hiked as well.
I've watched the kids play lots of sports…more than I care to tell.
Yes, we had many fun vacations throughout the USA,
And I've had the joy of music and have taught many how to play.

Some sad times also came along with loss of friends and family too,
And the floods we had in Harrisburg…
another challenge we went through.
So, yes, there have been hard times, for things weren't always great,
But overall, there's been much more that I appreciate.

We've had illnesses and surgeries that, of course, we hadn't planned,
But we also have been richly blessed, and that's been really grand.
The move we made to Ohio, the second time around,
Has provided years of friendships and a special church was found.

I haven't really talked much here of my beliefs and such
Because about a lot of this…I have already written much.
I have written about angels, prayer, and my deep faith in God
And how greatly this has helped me on the paths that I have trod.

My philosophy of life can be said in many ways:
"Cherish every moment and make the most of all your days."
"There is a destiny that makes us brothers; none goes his way alone.
All that we send into the lives of others comes back into our own."

Be a good steward of our planet and learn to live with all mankind,
For we are all so much alike…the more I travel, this I find.
Laugh and love and set your goals, then enjoy all that you do.
God has a plan for all of us… with His help, it will come true.

There are many plaques hung on my walls that tell of many things
That I have cherished through my life and the happiness they bring.
Places I have traveled and people I have met
And the joy of teaching music is one I can't forget.

The children and grandchildren and great grandchildren as well,
Have given us far more joy than we can ever tell.
I've traveled this world over and had many happy days.
Yes, I've "lived life to the fullest" and been blessed in many ways!

Inspirational Thoughts & Blessings

Blessings

Sometimes, I think, we all forget
To count the blessings that we get.
We may dwell on what's not right,
While all that's good slips out of sight.

If we would just enumerate,
We'd often find that our life's great.
Just take a little look around
And see the blessings that are found.
Then count those blessings every day
And thank God for them when you pray.
You'll find your troubles aren't as bad
As those that others may have had.

We all have days that aren't so good
When things don't go the way they should;
But "Keep the Faith," and persevere
And soon more blessings will appear.

For after rain, the sun comes through
And rainbows often follow too.
So "Count Your Blessings" one by one
And see the good things God has done.

How Do You Spend Your Time?

Do you spend some time with God each day?
Do you ask His guidance when you pray?
Do you listen then for what He'll say,
To help you, as you're on your way?

Do you read His Word to understand,
How best to live and what He's planned?
Do you praise and thank Him for what He's done,
For the gift He gave when He sent his Son?

Do you ask forgiveness and do you forgive?
Do you show His love in how you live?
Do you keep your mind on positive things
And look for the best, no matter what life brings?

Do you give tithes, time and talent too?
Do you further God's Kingdom with what you do?
Do you help others as Jesus would?
And do you encourage as you know you should?

Do you have faith that banishes fear,
So that your worries will disappear?
Do you trust the Lord with His plan for your life?
Do you share with Him your stress and strife?

We all have choices we can make each day
As to what we do and what we say.
Are your choices today the best they can be?
If you ask the Lord, do you think He'd agree?

Sometimes it's not easy, to do some of these things;
But the more that you do, the more joy it brings.
So again, let me ask, "How will you spend your day?
Will you thank God for His blessings and then follow His Way?"

Surprises

Let me say, first of all, that I love a surprise…
And the excitement and adventure it brings,
Like the wonders of nature, the song of a bird,
Or the thrill in the arrival of spring.
The unexpected phone call from a dear friend,
Who may just call to say "Hi;"
A card in the mail or some little gift,
Even the smile from those you pass by.

The love you receive in so many ways
That you might not feel you deserve,
The satisfaction and reward that you get
When you were really just trying to serve.
Isn't it a mystery how each day unfolds,
And often not at all like you plan?
It's amazing to me just what we can do
With God's help and deciding we can.

Now I know some may say, "Not all surprises are good,"
And I agree, 'cause I've had some that were bad,
But overall, I've been blessed with by far a lot more
Of those happy ones, instead of the sad.
And I think that most of us, if we're truthful, we'd say
That even though life "throws us a curve,"
Our blessings outweigh our misfortune, by far,
Maybe more than we really deserve.

Yes, life's full of surprises, and I cherish them all,
For it makes each new day more fun.
Just think for a bit…what would it be like
If we knew all the future from day one.

God Has a Plan

God has a plan for your life, in case you didn't know,
When things go well, it's often that He has made it so;
But what about when things aren't good,
Or things don't go the way they should?

Perhaps then we should re-assess
Just why it was that we weren't blessed.
Was it our choice that was so wrong?
Or was it a test to make us strong?

Sometimes when later we look back
We realize we've been "off-track",
That what God planned for us to do
We just weren't willing to pursue.

For we are each uniquely blessed
And many talents we possess.
Sometimes it takes a while to find
Exactly what God has in mind.

But rest assured, He has a plan,
And with His help you'll find you can
Do things you thought you never would
Or never really thought you could.

But when you've finally figured out
God's plan for you, you'll have no doubt
That this is what you're meant to do;
You'll feel fulfilled and happy too.

It's All about Love

If someone asks "What's the Bible about?"
It's all about Love, without a doubt!
For in the Bible, from beginning to end,
"Love" is the main message to be found, my friend.
Even in the beginning, when God formed our earth,
And when He gave us life, at the time of our birth…
It's all about Love.

When Jesus was asked, what's the most important part.
Even He said, "Love the Lord with all of your heart,"
And then, of course, He went on to say,
That we need to love our neighbor in the same way.
And when some asked who their neighbor would be,
The answer was really…anyone that we see.
It's all about Love.

Love is about caring and sharing with others.
Since we're the Lord's children, we are all brothers.
God so loved the world that His Son, He sent,
And it was for our sins that to the cross He went.
We read about Love and all the things love should be…
Like patient, kind, hopeful, and trustworthy.
It's all about Love.

Love's even greater than faith and hope too.
And Christ said, "Love each other, as I have loved you".
However, it's hard to explain all the Love verses, in rhymes;
For in the Bible, Love is mentioned more than 700 times!
Just remember that love should be part of all that you do,
And no matter what happens, God always loves you.
It's all about Love.

Do You Believe in Angels?

Do you believe in angels,
That they're messengers from above?
That they may come in many forms,
To show us of God's Love?

The Bible tells us many times…
By count, two hundred ninety-two,
About how angels will protect,
Guard, and guide all that we do.

Have you ever seen an angel?
Has one ever been your friend?
Did you know they are among us…
Often just around the bend?

Angels come in many ways…
Sometimes it's hard to see
Just who or what or why it was
Some angel came to be.

But later, if we will reflect,
God often makes it clear,
Exactly why He really sent
An angel to be near.

Have you ever wondered to yourself,
How is it that God knows
The perfect time to send them,
And where each Angel goes?

Some Angels must get very tired
And weary of their task,
For we do often test them
And so many Blessings ask.

You, too, can be an angel;
Sometimes you may not know
That what you've said or done today
God's love through you will show.

Yes, I believe in Angels,
For I know what they can do.
And if you will believe in them,
I'm sure they'll help you too.

"Life Is Fragile...Handle with Prayer"

This saying hangs upon my wall, and it reminds me every day
Of just how much it means to me, that I can always pray.
"Life is fragile, handle with prayer"...indeed, that is so true.
For I have found that prayer does help with everything I do.

Yes, life, I know, is fragile...and the flight of time is swift,
Every moment is so precious, and every day is such a gift!
How we handle all life's challenges is most important too,
And with prayer we have God's guidance in knowing what to do.

He not only gives you guidance but also peace of mind
And strength and inspiration, of a very special kind.
You know you always have a friend and that is special too,
And His love for you is endless, no matter what you do.

The promise of Eternal Life is His ultimate reward...
Indeed, prayer is a blessing that is given by our Lord.

Why Me, Oh God, Why Me?

Sometimes we ask, "Why me, oh God,"
When things go wrong, and there's a rough road to trod.
Is this trial to teach me something new
To bring me even closer to You?

When we're hurting, confused, depressed, and sad;
When our hopes have shattered and the outlook is bad,
It's so easy to blame and wonder 'why',
And it seems there's no way to justify.

Why did God choose me this burden to bear
When I've tried to do right, and I know that He cares?
When our world looks dark, and we're falling apart,
"Why me?", we wonder, down deep in our heart.

But what we so often forget to say,
Is 'Why me', when those good things are coming our way.
Why was I blessed and given so much,
When others I see have greater trials and such?

For God gives us friends and family, who help ease our pain.
He guides those who care for us 'till we're well again.
To stand steadfast when adversity arrives,
That is the challenge that helps us survive.

For these challenges we're given always help us grow…
Help us to see our weaknesses and how we need Him so.
He gives us strength for the course to stay,
And perhaps to do His work in a different way.

How easy it is to forget all He's done…
How He's given us so much, even His Son,
And how God continues His blessings to send;
How He heals all our hurts and is always our friend.

His Love is steadfast, and our faith must be too,
For He never fails us, no matter what we do.
He sends those who encourage and help us and care.
He gives joy and peace and answers our prayer.

Help us then, Lord, when things get tough
To remember that things soon won't be so rough.
That You're always there to heal, guide, and love,
And send more blessings to us from above.

So praise and thanksgiving is what we should say,
When things aren't going just our way,
And maybe, not 'Why me', but 'Why not me?' instead,
And then wait and see what His plan is ahead!

When Life Gives You Lemons

"When life gives you lemons…make lemonade," they say,
And that's a philosophy that I believe, to this day.
"Everything happens for a reason," is another quote too,
And when I look back upon life, I find this also true.

I first began painting after the '72 flood…
To fill frames when pictures were ruined by the mud.
It was something that I often thought I would do;
But just hadn't started…now I had reason to.

It proved to be great therapy in that stressful time,
A departure from the work of removing mud and slime.
If the floods hadn't happened, there were other things too,
That I might not have done or even learned how to do.

"Bloom where you're planted" is also good advice,
Since often, "life" doesn't plant us in a paradise,
But it depends on our outlook; that's really the key…
For we're usually as happy as we decide to be.

There are many more sayings that I've collected over time,
More than space allows or that I could even rhyme.
I've written elsewhere about some…so in closing, I'll just say…
"Cherish yesterday; Dream tomorrow, and Live today."

Choices

Our lives are filled with choices,
That we must make each day.
Sometimes, it may be easy,
Choosing what to do and say.
But some choices are not easy,
And wrong choices turn out bad.
Sometimes, in fact, the choice we make,
May make us feel quite sad.

Many times it's hard to know
Just what is best to do.
And even after choosing,
Then we question that choice too.
Yes, choices can be stressful,
And the worry may be great.
Maybe that's the reason
That we often hesitate.

But to worry doesn't help us.
In fact, it hinders too.
For what the worry is about,
Rarely does come true.
It really is a privilege
That a choice is ours to make,
And that we have the freedom…
Even though we make mistakes.

Remember we can always choose
Just how happy we will be;
Even when things don't turn out
The way we'd like to see.
And often we forget
That God is there to help us through
Those choices that we must make…
If we only ask Him to.

Each New Day

Each new day is a gift from God,
With dreams to fulfill and a new path to trod.
How you spend that day is your gift back.
Do you ask for His guidance and then stay on track?

Or do you ask; but then not do as He's willed;
And then wonder why you don't feel fulfilled?
Do you get caught up in the "hub-bub" of life:
The worry, the conflict, and all of life's strife?

Are you patient and loving, understanding and kind?
Or are you stressed and angry, with too much on your mind?
Do you forget that your Good Lord truly does care,
And that really He'll handle all this with your prayer?

Do you enjoy the roses, the sunrise, the sunset,
The beauty of nature…all the Blessings you get…
Friends and family, home, and even work too?
Do you really appreciate all the things you can do?

For how you spend this day, is yours to choose…
Will it be one that you'll cherish or just one that you lose?

Fruit of the Spirit

In the Bible, there's much written to guide us day by day;
Sometimes it's hard to comprehend and then to live that way.
There are "The Parables" that Jesus used, to help us understand
More about His teaching, as He walked about this land.
Then Paul wrote many letters to further make it clear
How we should act as Christians, if we really are sincere.

There are passages about the Holy Spirit 'Gifts' we can receive,
And words of reassurance, if we have Faith and will believe.
How we should treat our brothers as Christ himself would do;
How we can have Eternal Life through Christ…that's in there too.
And if the Holy Spirit we invite to dwell within,
The way becomes much easier and not so tempting then to sin.

The "Fruit" the Bible writes about, that too, the Lord will give.
Our challenge is to show that "Fruit" in the way in which we live.
LOVE, you notice, is the first and JOY then is the next;
After Joy comes PEACE…then PATIENCE follows in the text;
KINDNESS next and GOODNESS…also
FAITHFULLNESS, it's true,
GENTLENESS and SELF-CONTROL are listed in there too.

Yes, there are many guidelines written, to show us what to do;
The challenge then, for you and me, is how we follow through.
With all this guidance we receive…does it help us change our way?
Or do we simply read it , and then still live the same each day.
Dear Lord, you've richly blessed us…We give praise and
thanks to You.
We ask now, for strength and wisdom to honor You in all we do.

Spiritual Gifts

Do you ever wonder
Just how it is you'll know,
What "Special Gifts" God's given you
To help His Kingdom grow?

There is the gift of "Wisdom,"
And "Knowledge" is one too.
Even "Healing" and "Special Power"
Are among these gifts, it's true.

"Discernment" and "Interpretation"
And also "Prophecy."
Yes, we're each given different gifts
So that together, we're "One Body."

"Faith," you notice has been mentioned
In that Bible passage too;
And "Service"...that's the way to use
Those gifts He's given you.

Paul also writes of other gifts,
And in Corinthians, we read
How each fulfils a special place
In what God's Kingdom needs.

He writes of Faith and Hope and Love
Of this you may recall.
That's where it is he tells us,
That "Love" is greatest of them all.

So pray that you'll discover
The "Special Gifts" God's given you
And also ask His guidance
In how to use them too.

Prayer

The nice thing about prayer is
That you can pray anytime.
You needn't be in a church
Or any kind of shrine.

You can pray in the morning,
Even while in the shower...
At night while in bed,
Or just at any hour.

Prayer...what a great way
To talk with Our Lord!
It costs not a cent
And gives so much reward.

Prayer is for praising
And for thanking God too
For all the wonderful blessings
That He always gives to you.

What a marvelous gift
Our Lord has given....
That we can talk with Him here,
'Till we see Him in Heaven.

Friendship

What a wonderful gift to have a friend that will care;
A person with whom you can always share.
One who feels your joy and sorrow too.
One whom you know will be honest and true.
One who doesn't judge but accepts who you are.
One you can talk to, whether they're near or far.

A friend is one who will understand;
One that will lend a helping hand.
Yes, indeed, friendship is a great gift,
Especially when your soul needs a lift.
Someone to laugh with or cry a tear,
Someone who's there with a listening ear.

To have a friend, you must be one too,
And show love to others as Christ does to you.
For He is, of course, our one true friend--
The one on whom we can always depend.
Christ is the example of what friendship should be;
For he laid down His life for you and me.

Smile

A smile is such a simple thing,
For all the pleasure that it brings.
I find, so often, that it's true…
The smile you give comes back to you.

More muscles are required to frown…
To turn that smile upside down,
That makes it even more worthwhile,
Instead of frowning, just to smile.

And much in life is like that too
The things you give, come back to you,
Like love and friendship that you share,
Will soon return beyond compare.

Keep Smiling…

Music

Music…in my life, has played a great part.
The piano lessons, I loved right from the start.
It was when I was seven that I first started to play,
And I continue to teach and play to this day.

Music is a language that we all understand,
It can create feelings…majestic and grand;
Sometimes mysterious or sad it may be,
Or quiet and peaceful…there's such diversity.

Music can create any mood that you like,
It just depends on the chords that you strike.
It can express love, beyond what words say
Or relax and calm you, on a stressful day.

Music can paint pictures, to the listening ear,
And all sorts of images in one's mind might appear.
I've made many friends through music it's true
And experienced the joy of sharing music too.

Music is spiritual…a way to worship and pray
And commune with God in a special way.
When God gives us talents, even if they're not great;
To develop and share them we should not hesitate.

Oh, yes, it takes patience and work…sometime hard,
That, of course, is a factor that I can't disregard;
But the satisfaction derived once that process is done,
Outweighs the frustration, and it then becomes fun.

I hope you find music enjoyable too:
Whether singing or playing or whatever you do.
It could be in listening that you derive the most pleasure.
Music, indeed, is a pleasure to treasure.

Don't Give up!

When things don't go just the way that they should
And you think you've tried as hard as you could;
If you have an idea and have made a good plan,
Even though some folks won't think that you can,
Don't give up!

To persevere is not always easy to do,
But the reward is great when you follow through.
Set your goals high, then work hard to achieve;
If it's something you really and truly believe.
Never give up!

Throughout history most of the great things that were done
Required persistence for success to be won.
If something is worth doing, it's worth doing well,
And often that's harder to do than to tell,
But keep trying!

When the trail becomes steeper and the road is rough,
That's when "the tough get going," and you too can be tough.
Though dark clouds may hover and the rains may come,
The rainbow will follow and also the sun.
Remember God's promise!

Things often look darkest just before dawn,
But then in daylight you'll see how to go on.
If you have faith and trust in God's plan for you,
He'll give you the tools to carry it through.
Don't give up!

In Celebration of
Central College Presbyterian Church

The Church's One Foundation*

It was in 1843 that it all began,
With 19 members who followed God's plan.
For 17 years, they struggled until….
The 19 became 6…but with a strong will!
"Lock the doors", some said, "And walk away";
But those 6 said "No!", and decided to stay.

By 1870, the Chapel was done,
And that was the start of yet more things to come.
The Sanctuary was added; but that's not all…
The Educational Wing, Kirk and Ballard Hall,
The Academy and then the Buildings next door,
Now we have the challenge of a few acres more.

Through all these years many continued to strive
And faithfully gave to keep this Church alive.
From those first 19, Central College has grown,
In Mission and Outreach…we've made Christ's Love known
To those in the area and around the world too,
But there's always much more that we can do.

So now it's our turn to "Step up to the plate,"
And commit to the future before it's too late.
Like those before us, we need faith for this task,
But God always provides, if only we ask!
He gave strength and guidance to those years ago,
As they sought His Will to help His Church grow.

Through the ages, God's called many to follow His ways.
He called Moses to Mt Sinai, where he'd stay 40 days.
No, we won't go to Sinai, but in these next 40 days too,
We'll be seeking God's guidance for how best to do
This task set before us, that will help our Church grow.
Lord, bless us with courage, like they had long ago.

These first seven poems were written as part of "The Best Is Yet to Come" land purchase campaign at Central College Presbyterian Church.

Step out of the Boat!

Do you remember that old story, from the Bible, that we hear,
How Jesus walked on water and calmed the wind and fear?
When the disciples had been fishing and the wind began to blow,
And fear arose within them as their boat tossed to and fro.
Then suddenly they saw the Lord, walking toward their boat
And, of course, it made them wonder how He could stay afloat.

It was Peter, who then called out, "Lord, let me come to You,"
And as the Lord beckoned him, Peter walked on water too.
He walked, that is, until he took his eyes off of the Lord
And began to fear and wonder why he had stepped overboard.
Now when he started sinking, "Lord, save me," Peter shouted out,
And as the Lord caught Peter, he asked, "Why did you doubt?"

"Oh, you of little faith," Jesus then went on to say,
And sometimes, don't you wonder, if God thinks that of us today?
For when those "storms" come in your life, as, indeed, they do,
Does your faith in God sustain you or do you have doubts too?
If you "Step out of the boat," you'll find this to be true…
That God will calm the waters and then stretch His Hand to you.

If you keep your eyes on God and have faith to do His tasks,
He will then equip you…all you have to do is ask.
It does, indeed, take faith to live up to His plan,
But always what He asks of you…He helps, so that you can.
No, we needn't "walk on water"…our challenges are much less,
But if you take that "Step of Faith," you'll find that you'll be blessed.

By One Spirit

By One Spirit, we're joined together,
With other Christians in our life.
We share God's Love and fellowship,
We share joy and also strife.

Even Paul instructed Christians
Many years ago;
To be united by "One Spirit,"
So their Christian faith would grow.

Each has a gift that is unique,
And our talents differ too,
But that Christian Love unites us
In what God calls us to do.

So with that united Spirit,
Let us all go forth as one,
With the promise that Christ gave us…
"The Best Is Yet to Come"

Christ Knocks at the Door

We've often seen that painting,
Of Christ knocking at the door,
And, as you know, we have the option,
To either open or ignore.
If we open up that door,
Our lives will never be the same,
For the blessings that He'll give us
Will be more than we can name.

He may even give us challenges,
That we may feel we just can't do,
But He always gives the strength and guidance,
If we will only follow through.

Sometimes an opportunity
May not be given twice,
And sometimes it may seem to us
That it's quite a sacrifice,
For we may think it takes too much
Of our talent, time, or treasure,
But then we find when we look back,
The rewards were beyond measure.

So when Christ knocks at your door,
Will you invite Him to come in?
Or will you just ignore the knock,
And never know what might have been?

God Is in Control

In Proverbs we read, "Trust in the Lord'
And lean not on your own."
And if we will acknowledge that,
Then His plan He will make known.
The Bible, then, goes on to state,
That God will direct our way
If only we will trust in Him…
Then listen and obey.

Sometimes the way's not easy.
It may seem more than we can do;
But the thing we must remember,
Is that God always follows through.
Yes, it may take some sacrifice,
But you know He will provide,
For nothing is impossible,
When God is on your side.

Those who came before us
Must have prayed about their task,
But with God's help, they chose
To leave a legacy that will last.
You, too, can leave a legacy
Or not…it's up to you…
But if you put God in control,
He'll show you what to do.

Sacrifice

Sacrifice is a word that we sometimes hesitate to use;
For we may think that it involves something that we'll lose,
But sacrificial giving of your money, time, and talent too,
Will grow your faith and change your life in everything you do.

The Bible tells us that we'll reap whatever we will sow;
The more generous we are, the more our blessings grow.
God loves a cheerful giver; that's what we also read,
And we just can't out-give Him; He'll more than fill our need.

Our dear Lord sent His Son, who gave His life, that we might live;
That was the greatest sacrifice that He could ever give.
And yet all that God asks is that we have faith and will believe,
And if we do, Eternal Life is the gift that we'll receive.

No, to sacrifice is not easy; it's a challenge and a test.
It tests our faith and courage, but results are all the best.
When we are asked to sacrifice, we often hesitate;
And yes, it may be difficult, but the result, you'll find, is great.

Where your treasure is, that's where your heart will be;
According to the Scripture, you can't serve both God and money.
So just where is your treasure, and is your heart there too?
Do you have the faith to sacrifice and see what God will do?

Expect a Miracle

Miracles do happen to those who truly do believe,
And if we have the faith and pray, God's answer we'll receive.
For the blessings that God has for us, we only need to ask,
He is the Great Provider of what is needed for a task.
Now, in the Bible, often, we are shown that this is true;
But even folks of long ago, questioned their faith too.
And yes, we still have questions and wonder, "How can this be?"
For, to believe, is often hard, for the things we can not see.

Some use the term of "Miracle" in a sarcastic way,
When they think things won't happen, they might even say,
"Well, that would be a miracle"…and No, they don't believe
That it's a possibility to ever be achieved.
Sometimes we tend to question, even though we know God's Will.
We ask about the "how" and "when," without faith that He'll fulfill.
"Oh, ye of little faith", don't you think our Lord must say,
Because we've all seen "Miracles"…they happen every day

Remember we're God's hands on earth, to do all that we can,
To sometimes help with Miracles that He has in the plan.
Oh, it may mean some sacrifice, and He may put us to the test;
And if that happens, you can be sure, that you truly will be blessed,
For when we work together, it's amazing but so true,
How things begin to "fall in place" in what we're "called" to do.
So let's "Expect a Miracle" and let's prepare the way
For a Miracle to happen…Pray for it every day.

Isn't It Interesting How the Lord Works?

I remember how God tugged at my heart,
With yet another project, that I had no time to start;
But as I looked at the Hymnals in the Church pew,
They looked quite tattered, and it was not a nice view.
Now the church budget, usually runs in 'the red'
With no money for new ones, I thought, make covers, instead.
So I researched prices on yarn and all things we would need,
And found this could be done, for much less indeed.
But how would we cover them in a way that looked right?
One that would glorify God, when in sight.
And how would we attach them so they would stay?
And would people help to make them this way?

The next thing to do was to make a design.
A Christian cross was what first came into my mind.
But remember, I had never designed before,
So now a new challenge I had in store.
With God's help and guidance, I did manage this too.
Then as I viewed the hymnals, another thought came through…
If instead of just one design, it would be nice to see,
Maybe a couple different ones, or how about three?
Then there are 6 books in each row, so 6 would work too;
(Now remember, this was a project, I had no time to do)
But, as the ideas and designs continued to grow
I finally did 23 different designs for the rows.

Oh, yes, I'd done lots of needlework through the years,
But to create the designs, did bring some fears.
And how would I make the covers fit tight?
What yarn should be used and would the color be right?
If indeed, Christian crosses is what we would do,
Then we should explain the meaning of these crosses too.
So, I thought, I'll just get a book for what I need to know;
(For at that time, there were no computers, to look up "info.")
However, it took many hours to find these facts, it's true,
Then the next hurdle…how to attach, so they'll stick like glue.
With these and more problems solved, it seemed,
Next challenge was to find a "Stitching Team."
But at the first workshop, there were such a few,
That many had doubts about what we could do;
But, you know, when the Lord gives you 'A Plan'
He makes things happen, so that you can
Accomplish those things that you never would,
Things that many thought you never could.
Well, the numbers grew and we stitched and had fun
And 18 months after this project was begun,
We dedicated 650 covers in March of 1989,
To the Glory of God!…(and the covers looked fine.)

Then other churches ask for the way
To make these covers, so I decided one day
To write a book of instructions, telling just what to do,
Which we then sold and made money for church missions too.
And a copyright, later, I actually received,
Since patterns like this , no one else had achieved.
We had fun and fellowship along the way
And developed friendships, that continue today.
Folks from 9 to 90, and from in other places too,
Saw us stitching and asked what they could do.
One older member, who really was blind,
Found even she could do something of this kind.

Of course there are many details, that I've left out,
And perhaps you're wondering, what this is all about.
It's much more than these covers that we lovingly made;
It's to tell when God gives you a task, don't be afraid.
For He never asks about your ability, you know,
Only, availability, and "the Seed" He will sow.
He'll make time in your schedule, no matter how stressed,
And the rewards you'll reap, are always 'The Best'!
Yes, isn't it interesting, the way things work out?
How God plants ideas that you had not thought about?
How these things may bring others to know Jesus too,
As you show Christ's love, in what He's "called" you to do.

Trust in the Lord

Trust in the Lord with all your heart, and lean not on
your own understanding; in all your ways,
acknowledge him, and He will make your paths straight.
Proverbs 3: 5-6

Trust in the Lord, this passage says,
And trust with all your heart;
Not after all your plans have failed;
But trust Him from the start.
Trust Him every day in every way,
And your path He will make straight.
Without that faith and trust in Him,
The path is hard to navigate.

For life is filled with challenges
And decisions we must make.
Do you sometimes find those challenges,
Almost more than you can take?
Don't forget, God's there for you,
No matter what the task,
If only you remember,
All you need to do, is ask.

He always gives the choice…
To seek Him, or not…it's up to you;
But I know that this you will find
That you'll be blessed, if you do!
What blessed reassurance
That this can give each day,
To know that He's there waiting,
Just to hear you when you pray.

Prayer:
Dear Lord, I thank you, that you are always with me.
In Jesus name, I pray.   Amen.

Ellsworth Chapel Dedication

In 1843, when it all began,
There were 19 members, who followed God's plan.
For 17 years, they struggled, until…
The 19 became 6, but with an 'iron will',
"Lock the doors", some said, "and walk away";
But the 6 said, "No", and decided to stay.

It was in 1870, when this chapel was done,
And they met, to thank the Almighty One.
Now, through the years, many persevered here,
And this church has grown, through much sweat and tear.
Then in 1958, the Ellsworths came,
Dick and Linda, to actually call them by name.

And here they stayed, more than 35 years.
They helped turn tears into smiles and cheers.
So the 19 became 3000 and more,
And, who knows what else God has in store.
This little chapel, now redone,
Is very special to each and every one.

We know, Dick, you've liked it right from the start,
So that's why this honor, we'd like to impart.
As of the 19th of December, 1993,
The 'Ellsworth Chapel', this church will be.
We honor you, "Rev," with this dedication,
To show you our love and appreciation.

And also to Linda, we say "Thank You"…
Even Pam, Penny, Peter, Beth, and Jennifer too.
To Central College, you've all given much
Time, talent, love, and that special touch.
We just pray Central College will continue to grow,
And that our love of Christ Jesus, always will show.
May this Ellsworth Chapel long endure,
And may it always be "With an open door."

The Dedication of the Pre-School Wing
of
Central College Presbyterian Church on
April 23, 1993
to Linda Wells Ellsworth

As Pre-School Director for so many years,
You've taught many children and wiped many tears.

Since '71, how our Pre-School has grown,
As all of our records clearly have shown.

With love and compassion, patience and care,
Your guidance and knowledge, you'd always share.

Friend, teacher, wife, mother...all "hats" fit you fine.
No matter the task, you always found time.

So, now on this day, we would like to acknowledge,
On behalf of the Session and your own Central College,

All that you've done and continue to do,
By dedicating this Pre-School Wing to you.

A Tribute to "Rev"
on his 35th Year as Pastor at Central College Church--1993

We all have been blessed, in so many ways,
And it is to the Lord that we give all the praise.
But you're one of our blessings, all members will say
When He sent you to us to show us the way.
The guidance you've given, encouragement and care,
And the Love of Jesus, that you've taught us to share;
The years with us, we do truly treasure,
The lives you've touched are too many to measure.
It's been 35 years; but there's even more,
And we're all looking forward to what's yet in store!

A fitting tribute is so hard to give,
But perhaps we can, in the way that we live.
So may Central College continue to grow,
And may all of us, let our lights always glow.
May each heart be touched to show others 'the way'.
It's for this Divine Guidance that we continue to pray,
And in our so doing, may you always know,
That you had much to do with the way that we go.

A Tribute to the Rev. Dr. Richard D. Ellsworth
In Celebration of 40 Years as Pastor of
Central College Presbyterian Church—1998

Some call you, "Richard"; to others you're "Rev"
Or maybe some know you as "Dr. Ellsworth" instead.
You answer to "Dick"…you're our Pastor and friend,
And this is the tribute that we'd like to extend.

When you were an engineer, you were called by the Lord
To change your career and go preach "the Word."
It was in '58, to Central College you came,
But it took three "Calls" before you'd remain.

You have, indeed, blessed us, more than we ever can say,
With your messages on Sundays and in your life every day.
You've inspired and challenged, enlightened and led,
Encouraged and guided…what more can be said?

You're an example, a leader, and a teacher, it's true,
And your love for the Lord always shines through.
From that first congregation of 200 or so
To more than 3000, we continue to grow.

From the days in the chapel (which was once to be closed)
To the Sanctuary and Ballard…and still on it goes.
The Educational Wing came and then later, Kirk Hall,
The Pre-School was started, then the Academy this fall.

And much of the reason, it can truly be said,
Is because of the way, you've so effectively led.
Forty years is a long time, and you've given so much…
We can't even count all the lives that you've touched!

For it's not just the buildings; it's the Mission we share,
To lead others to Christ and to show them we care.
Central College must surely have been God's Call for you,
And we want to say, that it's our choice for you too.
May you continue to be richly blessed even more,
For who knows what the Good Lord still has in store?
So with friendship and love from us…one and all,
We THANK YOU, Dick Ellsworth, for answering God's Call.

"Building Our Faith" Ground Breaking

It all started with a "Step of Faith" about three years ago.
We now continue with that faith to help our Mission grow.
Some of these 'Steps' are now complete, and soon this will be too.
We give all thanks and praise to God for help in what we do.

We know if those who came before, weren't willing to commit
To give and go that 'extra mile', rather than to quit,
Then our Mission and this Ministry would not have been the same;
So now it's up to us to give and continue in His Name.

We have learned of Christ's commission—to do His work each day,
To bless all those as we've been blessed, perhaps this is one way.
So on this October 27th, in the year 2002,
We gather to continue some work that's yet to do.

We ask a special blessing, Lord, as we break ground today.
May what we are about to build please You in every way.
Guide and direct our work, Dear Lord, and give us visions new,
That this might be a vessel for Your Love to travel through.

In Recognition of the 45Th Anniversary
of the Ordination
of the Rev. Dr. Richard D. Ellsworth on This Day,
November 30, 2003

It was to Central College that he had been called,
And here was ordained and duly installed,
On the 30th of November, 45 years to this date,
In the year of Our Lord—1958.
He came in the snow, with wife, Linda and four,
Then later their children would number one more.

Some call him 'Richard', to others he's 'Rev',
And he answers to 'Dick' or 'Dr. Ellsworth' instead;
But whatever the name, he's our Pastor and friend,
A teacher, a leader—the list has no end.
He's a counselor, a chaplain, and serves lots of Boards;
Even does mission trips—truly serving the Lord.

Forty-five years is a long time, and he's given much;
We can't even count all the lives that he's touched.
He really has blessed us in so many ways
With his message on Sunday and his life every day.
He has inspired and challenged, enlightened and led,
Encouraged and guided—what more can be said!

From that first congregation of 200 or so,
Now almost 3000 and we continue to grow.
From those days in the Chapel (which was once to be closed),
To the Sanctuary and Ballard and still on it grows;
The Education Wing was added and later Kirk Hall,
The Pre-school, the Academy, then the new building this fall.

Much of the reason for this growth, it is said,
Is because of his vision and the way he has led.
But the buildings mean nothing without purpose, that's clear.
It's the Christian outreach and fellowship year after year.
It's the teaching and sharing God's Love here and there
And it's showing that love in the way that we care.

So with Congratulations and love from us—one and all
We thank you, Dick Ellsworth, for answering God's "Call."

For the Celebration of "Rev's" Service
February 11, 2007

What an honor and privilege it is to be here today,
To commemorate "Rev's" service in this special way.

It was 30 years ago that our family moved here,
And what a blessing to find this church so near.

On that first church visit, we decided to stay...
A very wise choice...I can truthfully say.

The friendship and love, the nurture and care,
And "Rev's" marvelous messages are beyond compare.

For the past 20 years, I've been an Elder and Clerk,
So I've been privileged to see "Rev's" untiring work.

I've often remarked that I can best say
What's in my heart, in a rhyming way,

But this poem, however, was a challenge for me;
For there's so much to tell....I think you'd agree.

I've tried to be brief and hopefully not bore,
Or repeat things that I've written for occasions before.

So the following poem I now dedicate and commend
As a tribute to you, "Rev," our Pastor and friend.

A Special Tribute to
The Rev. Dr. Richard D. Ellsworth,
Our Pastor and Friend

When you came to Central College many years ago,
God truly blessed our congregation—this we know.
You've been such an inspiration throughout all these years.
We've shared in joy and sorrow, with laughter and with tears.
You helped us understand God's Word by your messages and deeds.
Together, with our missions, we've helped others with their needs.

Our congregation is much larger than when you came in '58.
The Preschool and Academy were started since that date.
Now there are many buildings that have been added too—
Making room for all those things that we at Central College do.
It's your vision and your guidance that have led us in this way,
And your untiring efforts, which continue to this day.

How can we ever thank you for all these things you've done?
This poem just can't be long enough to list them every one.
You have touched so many lives and so faithfully have served,
There's just no tribute we can give that's as much as you deserve.
Please do remember, that we love you and your family too.
You've all been special in our lives, with everything you do.

Many prayers have been said and more are prayed each day,
Thanking God that He sent you to minister in this way.
"No one ever served a finer church", is often what you've said,
But "No one's had a finer pastor" is what we'd say instead.
We have many cherished memories; indeed, that is so true,
And we pray continued blessings on all that you will do.

I'm Glad to Be at Central College Presbyterian Church

I'm glad to be at Central College and I'd like to tell you why,
There are really lots of reasons, so I'll try to clarify.
It's the people and the pastors and all that happens here;
It's the fellowship and love—it's even fun to volunteer.
It's the caring and the sharing in the good times and the bad,
For friends make good times better and the bad times, not so sad.
When we sing and pray together and we seek to learn God's Will,
There's a bond that seems to happen then and that bond continues still.

Now it doesn't help your diet here, for we always seem to eat,
But this church does help feed your Soul, and that's the part that's neat.
"Oh, this church is just too big", you may have heard some say,
But I've found that when you get involved, the "bigness" goes away.
It's a joy to come on Sunday to hear the message and much more,
To feel so welcome and accepted—for this church has an "open door"
That anyone can enter and no one will question why,
Because to walk that 'narrow path' is hard, but we're all here to try.

Have you ever stopped to ask yourself, why is it that you came?
And if you did, I'll bet you too, would find a lot the same.
It may be for the music or the class that you attend,
Or maybe it's to worship or to see that special friend.
You see the reasons are so many that I've touched on just a few,
And the rest I'll leave because I know that you will add some too.
I feel so blessed, that in God's plan, I think He led me here,
And the blessings of this fellowship just grow year after year.

Stewardship*

God has richly blessed me, as I'm sure He has you too,
And all He asks us in return, is help with work He has to do.
Stewardship is our response, for all that God has done.
It's our commitment to His work, as taught us by His Son.
To give or tithe is to commit to the church and to our Lord.
It's really such a simple thing, and it's according to His Word.
Without a pledge, it's difficult. I think you will agree;
It's hard to know what can be done or what the plans can be.
If Christ had not declared the love He has for you and me;
If He'd not fulfilled His promise, then I wonder where we'd be.

How can we not declare then, what we will try to do
And commit to His work faithfully in all that we pursue?
A 'Declaration of Intent' is to pledge a part of what we earn.
And God replaces that, with much more, as you will learn.
Of course, there may be many, thinking: "Oh, here we go again…
Always hearing about giving, instead of being saved from sin."
But, if we give as we've been blessed, what a change there'd be,
Not only in this church…but the whole community.
So give according to your heart and what the Lord has done.
Just remember how He gave when He sacrificed His Son.

Written for Stewardship Sunday at Church 1996

The Bakeless Bake Sale*

We call this a "Bakeless Bake Sale"…
The best part is…you needn't bake.
No need to clutter up the kitchen,
Or even wonder what to make.
You don't need to run out to the store,
Or try to find that recipe.
Instead, we've tried to make this,
Just as easy as can be.

You can write a check for the amount
That you feel you can give,
To help support our Missions,
Both away and where we live.
All the money that you donate
Is used in just this way;
For as "Presbyterian Women",
We gladly serve…and without pay.

Some money goes to feed the hungry,
Heal the sick or help the poor.
Some goes to spread the Gospel,
And we could really list much more.
So if you choose to be a part
Of this Mission work we do,
Then in the envelope, enclose a check
To "Presbyterian Women"…and we THANK YOU.

Written for on-going missions at the Church

Prayer Shawl Blessing*

This shawl was made with LOVE and PRAYER,
To show you how much others CARE.
And to remind you of GOD'S LOVE
That He gives freely from above.

May it surround you with WARMTH and PEACE,
And STRENGTH and HOPE that never cease.
May it give you COURAGE for each new day,
And a SPECIAL JOY—all this we pray.

Written for on-going missions at the Church

The Joy of Dolls*

When you think of your childhood, what was your favorite toy?
For many it's often a doll that brought joy.

If that doll could talk, rather than sit on a shelf,
What wondrous tales might she tell of herself?

Would she tell of the hands that first brought her home,
The hands that would dress her and hair gently comb?

She could probably tell how someone gave her a name,
How they'd have tea parties and perhaps play a game.

Maybe they'd read a story or sing "Rock-a-Bye",
And they'd cuddle and comfort when she was hurt or would cry.

Those hands may have been little and could not do things well,
But oh, how they loved her, of this she could tell!

And sometimes it might be that she'd comfort them too,
If they'd had a bad day or were home with the flu.

She might tell how they played "pretend" or went for a walk,
Or how often it was such fun to just sit and talk.

** The following three poems were written for
Mother-Daughter Luncheons with these themes*

Today our lifestyle may be far from this doll,
But the things that she tells here still affect us all.

For we do need to care, to show love, to have joy,
But now with each other instead of a toy.

Perhaps it's God's way of having us learn
To nurture each other, to show our care and concern.

For the lessons learned on our dolls and then our friends too,
Are important in life, in whatever we do.

That acceptance and truthfulness—no fake or façade,
But genuine love—unconditional and broad.

The joy and excitement of each new day,
Dear Lord, help us always to feel that way.

Tell Me a Story

"Tell me a story", the little one said.
"Tell me a story, before I go to bed."
And many a parent has lovingly told,
Those beautiful Bible stories of old.
Tales about Noah and that awesome ark;
Or how God's always with us, even in the dark.

There are many stories, that we all love to hear.
Like David and Daniel, who showed no fear.
How about Jonah and that great big whale,
Or little Moses, put in the basket to sail.
There are stories of Martyrs and Saints and Kings;
Stories of battles and all sorts of things.

Remember the story of how Jesus fed
Thousands of people with five loaves of bread?
And then how Moses parted that Sea;
And short little Zacchaeus climbed up that tree.
Now Job had his problems and Thomas his doubt,
Samson was strong 'till Delilah found out.

Tales of the Good Shepherd and how He cared for His sheep;
That always gave comfort and helped one get to sleep.
But one of the best stories, I think you'll agree,
Was when Jesus said, "Let the children come unto me".
And whether we're little or old as a sage,
The comfort He gives us depends not on age.

So let's tell this story again and again;
Of how Jesus loves us and died for our sin.
And how He's our comfort, shelter, and guide;
And how, in His love, we can always abide.
Yes, tell me that story, for it never grows old!
Again, tell me that story, even though I've been told.

Hats, Hats, Hats

How many "Hats" have you worn in your life?
The "Hat" of a mother, a daughter, a wife?
A sister, a grandma, a teacher, a nurse?
A student, an actress, a writer of verse?

Perhaps in an office you work or a store,
You could be a doctor, a lawyer…there are choices galore:
A waitress, a chemist, or an engineer,
A musician, a model, or a volunteer.

Each day you may do one of these jobs and six more…
It may be to chauffer, to clean, or to go to the store;
To perhaps be a friend who lends a helping hand,
Someone who will listen and understand.

Do you minister to those who have a need?
So often that's where you can plant a "seed"
For this "Hat" is much more than a thing on your head.
It's who you are, what you do, or perhaps what you've said.

God gives you talents and blessings no end;
How you live each day, is the "message" you send…
For some may be looking to you for a goal,
And perhaps that 'someone' is a lost soul.

So put on your "Hat"…whatever it may be,
Do your best and wear it proudly, for all to see!
Ask the Good Lord's guidance, in all that you do,
And let the light of Christ's love always shine through.

Yes, the "Hats" that you wear may be many indeed…
Do the ones that you wear, sow the right "seed"?

The Central College Presbyterian Church Quilt

*Designed to commemorate the 150th Anniversary
of the founding of this church
1843-1993
Lovingly given by the Presbyterian Women
Dedicated to the Glory of God
February 13, 1994*

This Quilt represents what we'd like to tell,
About Our Heritage, Our Worship, and fun times as well.
Whether it be in Music, Study, Dinners, or Prayer,
In Mission or Outreach—it's the Fellowship we share.

Celebrations, Memorials, Christian Symbols and such;
There's a list of the Pastors, who've given so much.
Evangelism, Retreats, and Activities galore,
Please look closely to see that there's also much more.

May this quilt be a witness of our Faith, Hope, and Love,
And a constant reminder of our dear Lord above.
May it be a tribute to those gone before
And an inspiration to all who will pass through our door.

This Quilt was done by many women who shared
Their talent and time, because they really cared.
And it's hoped that the work of their hands will convey
How God richly blesses us all every day.

A Challenge of Service*

We've heard about the service of many women long ago,
And that service still continues, as many of you know.
But it's not only up to women to serve the Lord this way—
For everyone can be of service in many ways each day.

How can "I" serve, perhaps you ask—What gift have I to share?
The talents that I have are few, and there's just no time to spare.
There may be others here, as well, to do what needs be done,
So why should I agree to help, 'cause I'm sure they'll get someone.

But think of how the world would be, if no one would volunteer
To be the hands and heart of God for all His children here.
No one to teach or show the way; no one to dry a tear;
No one to feed the hungry; heal the sick or quiet fear;
No one to lend a helping hand or encourage with a prayer;
No one to do those special things to show someone they care.

Each one of us can be of service in our own Church and far beyond,
For there are many ways to serve the Lord---we need only to respond.
I have a plaque that's in my home, and this is how it reads—
"God asks not of our ability—availability is what He needs."

Yes, there are many ways that we can serve, for each has a gift unique.
We may wonder where or how to serve—sometimes we need to seek.
Our God has given many gifts; His Son, of course—the best,
But He's given other gifts as well—We all are truly blessed!

And when we read the Scriptures, we find that tells us more,
That we are "Blessed to be a Blessing'" and to help the sick and poor.
We speak of Service here today, for that's one of God's Gifts too,
And there are many ways to serve Him—many things that we can do.
"For in as much as we have done, unto one of the least of these,
We've also done it unto God"—and when we do, I'm sure He's pleased.

There's another little poem, that perhaps you've even heard,
It's just another way of saying what's written in God's word,
For it also speaks of Service, and the message is quite clear,
So I hope that you will listen, as I share it with you here.
"There is a destiny that makes us brothers, none goes his way alone.
All that we send into the lives of others, comes back into our own!"

There also is a Scripture that I'm sure you've read before---
That says it's hard to "out-give" God, for the return is always more!
There's so much joy in serving God—the rewards just can't compare;
For what comes back into our lives, is far more than what we share!

The Challenge then to each one of us—men, women, children too,
Is to find a way to serve our God each day in what we do!

This poem was written for a worship service presented by the Presbyterian Women

Our Mission as Presbyterian Women

To nurture, support, work, and build,
And with the Holy Spirit be filled;
To strengthen and witness; be faithful and care;
Forgive and pray; study and share
With our Sisters in Christ…both here and afar;
To bring peace and justice wherever we are.
These are the things we commit ourselves to,
As Presbyterian Women, in whatever we do.

People & Places
Beyond the Familiar

Travel

To travel, I find, enlightens one's mind
About peoples and cultures of a different kind,
And perhaps if we tried to understand others more,
There would be more peace and a lot less war.
I wonder sometimes why we can't see the need
To care more for this world with our every deed;
To value its treasures that we have in our care;
To savor the beauty, to protect it and share
So the generations that follow will be able to see
All of God's Great Creation, as He meant it to be.

Countries Visited

AFRICA
Botswana
Egypt
Kenya
Morocco
Namibia
South Africa
Tunisia
Zimbabwe

ANTARCTICA

ASIA
China-[2x]
Hong Kong-[2x]
India
Israel
Japan-[2x]
Malaysia-[2x]
Nepal
Russia
South Korea
Singapore-[2x]
Syria
Thailand-[2x]
Turkey
Vietnam

AUSTRALIA and OCEANIA
Fiji
Queensland
New S. Wales
New Zealand

EUROPE
Austria-[3x]
Belgium
Bulgaria
Croatia
Czech Republic
Denmark
England-[4x]
Finland
France-[3x]
Germany-[3x]
Gibraltar
Greece
Greenland
Hungary-[2x]
Iceland
Ireland
Italy-[3x]
Liechtenstein
Luxembourg
Monaco
Netherlands-[4x]
Norway-[2x]
Poland
Portugal
Romania
Scotland
Serbia
Slovakia-[2x]
Spain-[2x]
Sweden
Switzerland-[2x]
Turkey
Vatican
Wales

NORTH AMERICA
Canada
  [Most all
  Provinces]

Central America
  Costa Rica-[2x]
  Guatemala
  Honduras
  Mexico-[2x]
  Panama-[2x]

United States
  [All 50 States]

SOUTH AMERICA
Argentina
Brazil
Chile-[2x]
Columbia
Ecuador-[2x]
Paraguay
Peru
Uruguay

ISLANDS
Antique
Aruba
Bahamas
Barbados
Bermuda
Capri
Cayman-[2x]

Dominica
Falkland
Galapagos
Gotland
Jamaica
Macau
Madeira
Majorca
Martinique
Mykonos
Patmos
Prince Edward
Puerto Rico
Rhodes
San Blas
Sicily
St. John
St. Kitts
St. Lucia
St. Maarten
St. Martin
St. Thomas
Tortola
Virgin Gorda

. . . and still traveling

Enjoying the Journey

Life is a journey, and to each one it's unique.
We all have desires and different things that we seek.
Who we are and even what we will become,
In part, depends on the things we have done.
Sometimes our ultimate goal gets in the way
Of just "Enjoying the Journey" of each new day.

Along this road that we travel in life
There may be challenges, struggles, and strife,
But in these times too, if we really try,
We can learn and grow, then understand why.
Was it because our choices were not really the best
Or did it make us stronger? Was that the test?

Whatever the reason, usually after a while,
We can often look back and then perhaps even smile.
When we realize that how much we've really been blessed
Is so much more than all the things that caused stress.
So let's "Enjoy the Journey," whatever it brings,
For life is too short to worry about things.

Besides, what we worry about usually never comes true,
And if it does, there may not be much we can do.
If we just do our best…whatever that may be,
And make the most of all our ability,
Then trust in the Lord, and "Live Life" each day
We'll then "Enjoy the Journey" along life's highway.

Travel and Grow

Traveling has given me such exciting delights,
To see places read about and beautiful sights;
To learn different cultures and see life from their view,
To meet people, live history and taste exotic menus;
To climb the pyramids or take a trip down the Nile,
To see lions on safari or Australian crocodile,
To cruise on the Seine or the huge Amazon,
Or ride camels and elephants…the adventures go on.

Cathedrals and castles or palaces grand,
Museums and gardens…"Wonders" cover the land;
Seas and oceans filled with such colorful things,
Balloon rides and rafting…what a thrill that all brings!
Whale watching in Mexico, trekking in Nepal,
Concerts in Vienna or in the Alps a snowfall,
Iguanas in the Galapagos and in Alaska, caribou,
Orchids in Singapore, Fiji and Hawaii too;

Ruins in Italy or prayer at Jerusalem's wall;
Antarctic penguins or magnificent waterfalls;
Pandas in China; in Japan, temples and shrines;
Stone walls in Ireland…quaint villages on the Rhine;
Tigers in India and the Taj Mahal too;
Elephants in Thailand, and they're not in the zoo;
Monkeys on Gibraltar and windmills in Spain;
Flowers in Amsterdam…in Brazil, jungles and rain.

Machu Picchu is awesome on the Inca trail in Peru,
And crossing the Canal in Panama is intriguing too.
Even Liechtenstein and Luxembourg are small but unique,
And the people in New Zealand are outnumbered by sheep.
Iceland and Greenland are both interesting scenes,
But most of Greenland is ice and much of Iceland is green.
In Greenland the Inuits live by the ice-covered bays,
And I'll remember riding that dog sled for the rest of my days!

In contrast, there's the Caribbean, with beaches galore;
Rain forests and waterfalls...even caves to explore,
Sugarcane fields and monkeys in trees,
Tropical flowers and beautiful blue seas;
Then there's Bulgaria, Croatia and Hungary too,
And lots more along the Danube (and that river's not really blue).
These contrasts in countries are always exciting to see:
Some have hot deserts...others are cold as can be.
The people are different, and yet we're all much the same,
Sometimes differing only in language and name.

In Greece, the Acropolis and the Mediterranean Sea;
Turkish coffee with Bedouins...in Morocco, mint tea;
Scandinavia and Russia are interesting as well;
Each is a contrast with a different story to tell.
Cruising the rivers, canals, lakes and seas;
Enjoying the ports, the food, the ocean breeze;
Going by plane, bus, train, car, ship or van...
Sometimes just getting there anyway that you can.

The U.S. is a good place to get started first,
For all fifty states are so very diverse.
Big cities, small towns, farmland and seashore,
Mountains and canyons...wildlife by the score.
It's not possible, however, to list all the places in rhyme,
For that would take far too much of your time,
But I hope I've inspired you to travel and grow,
For it's such a big world with lots of places to go.
Travel makes you appreciate what you have here at home
And will hopefully inspire you to continue to roam.

Egypt and the Nile

How exciting it was to take a trip down the Nile,
For I had wanted to do this for quite a long while.
It was like looking back in time over thousands of years,
And seeing things I'd read about suddenly appear.
Life was much slower paced and had more primitive ways..
That was how these folks spent most of their days.
Donkey carts and oxen were used in their chores,
And sugar cane and date palms grew by the shores.

The Nile is the life-line in this climate dry and hot;
But with primitive irrigation they create a lush spot.
Even from the plane, one could see a green space
On each side of the Nile wherever water was placed.
Gigantic temples and statues soon came into view,
And there were museums filled with antiquities too.

I rode a camel across the hot desert sand,
And then climbed a pyramid…the view there was grand.
Inside that pyramid it was dark, hot, and steep,
And one had to bend low and sometimes just creep.
The air there was stuffy and seemed old, as well,
Oh, the stories those walls could probably tell.

We viewed gold from King Tut and the Valley of Kings,
In the Cairo Museum, there were unbelievable things.
The streets in Cairo were chaotic, that's true,
With cars, donkeys, buses…and not just a few.
No lanes marked for traffic and each found their own way
Even bicycles and walkers…what an array!

I had mint tea in the "Souk", which is their market place,
And everything imagined was sold in this space.
Live produce, gold jewelry, spices galore,
Clothing, antiques, wooden carvings, and much more.
It was fun to bargain for things they had made,
Then both seller and buyer felt it was a fair trade.

There was even a wedding in our hotel one night,
With Egyptian folk music and an unforgettable sight:
Belly dancers with lit candles on top of their head.
To our way of thinking…a strange way to be wed.
The folks there were friendly and interesting to meet;
Yes, visiting this country was really a treat.

Travels in the Holy Land

What a privilege, I thought, to share my insight,
About our Holy Land trip, when they asked me to write.
"Write a poem," someone said, "about what you know".
But an inspiration, I need, before the words flow.
To visit the Holy Land, was an inspirational delight…
I still get some Goosebumps, even now as I write!
To step back in time, in such sacred land…
Touched my soul deeply, like the touch of God's hand.

Great contrasts there were, of the old and the new…
Donkeys beside autos…to name just a few.
Nomads still living in a wilderness dry,
As though 4000 years had never passed by.
Here are some places that I recall…
I'll name just a few…certainly not all.

In Jaffa, it was there that Jonah set sail,
And Peter was there too…remember that tale?
The Valley of Adjalon, where the sun stayed high;
Qumran Caves and Masada, with the Dead Sea near by.
On the Isle of Patmos, John received inspiration
To write that great Book…it's called Revelation.
Places Paul preached were of interest too….
Athens, Rhodes, and Ephesus…to name a few.
There were the Dead Sea Scrolls of 2000 years;
And Tombs of the Prophets, of Jesus, and His peers.

In Gethsemane Garden where He went to pray,
The same Olive Trees still remain to this day.
A moment remembered…no, I'll never forget,
How it felt to pray, where Christ prayed and wept.
There was Shepherds Field and the Nativity Site
We sang carols by the manger…what a delight!
Mt. Zion and Moriah, where He lived and talked…
Yes, I walked that day, where Jesus walked.

In Old Jerusalem, at the Temple Wall,
I went to pray, and I still recall
How it felt to stand in such a place,
With all faiths and creeds and colors of face.
How we all prayed together, to the same Holy One;
Whether called Allah, Jehovah, or Jesus, His Son.
In the cracks of that wall, all prayers remain
On paper that's folded and pressed-in with great strain.
So the names of my family, my friends, and my church too
Are still there being blessed…each day anew!

What a privilege, I said, when I started this rhyme,
To share such an experience…Thanks for your time.
I hope you'll remember when this poem is complete,
More than this journey, though the places were "neat,"
That God and His Love will never cease, falter, or rest;
His blessings are endless, His reward is the best!
May God richly bless you and give peace to your strife,
And may His Love shine through you all the days of your life!

Medical Mission to Honduras

We began this trip on a dark rainy day,
To Honduras, where for a week we would stay.
There were eight in our group, as we waited to start
At the airport, our flight was late to depart.
In Houston, it was, that we met two more
Of our Medical Brigade to help the sick and the poor.
With our orange shirts blazing, for that was our wear,
We were on our way to show these folks that we care.

"Making God's Love Visible" is what our shirts read,
And we hoped to do that everywhere we were led.
This was a "Vacation with a purpose" for everyone,
With a mission to show God's Love, in what's done.
We all arrived safely, to the place where we'd stay,
But our medical supplies, didn't come 'till next day.
So we went into La Ceiba to shop around
And see what souvenirs could be found.

We attended a local church that Sunday night
And were warmly welcomed, to our delight.
The Coco Pando, was the place where we stayed
And traveled from there each day on Brigade.
"Pando", they told me, means "crooked road"
And "Coco" means "coconut", so I've been told.
What a beautiful setting…this place by the sea
With surrounding mountains and tropical trees.

The beach there was littered with rocks and debris,
And no one swam here, in the polluted sea.
Herds of cattle would pass by on the beach,
On the way to a pasture that they hoped to reach.
Very early each morning, I'd sit by the sea,
And as the sun rose, what tranquility there'd be.
Occasionally, a rooster would herald the day,
Like he was making a call for the sun to obey.

The tide had gone out and left a high water mark
Along with some other things washed up in the dark.
The little sand crabs had gone back to bed,
Now only their holes could be seen there instead.
Have you ever noticed, when you watch the sun rise,
How each moment it changes those beautiful skies?
The waves tumble in with their greeting, as well.
What adventurous tales, I'll bet these waves could tell!

The clouds, ever changing, float peacefully by,
Sometimes in a race, across the sky.
Sea birds are busy, skimming the water for prey,
Yes, the rise of the sun, also starts their day.
Sometimes even objects, that I barely could see,
Would cross the horizon in front of me.
Then clouds, in strange shapes, would form in the sky,
And mysterious images would then fill my eye.

Driftwood and rocks laid at water's edge,
Some places they formed an unusual hedge,
Like they were keeping the sea within its bounds
And protecting the sand and nearby grounds.
A pelican would pass with the flapping of wing,
Just looking for any edible thing.
Sometimes the sea just looked like glass,
But in just a short while that too would pass.

The sea is always changing, as our lives are too,
And each day there's a chance to start fresh and new.
We just need to take time to really pause, look, and see
All God's wondrous world and the great diversity.
From the sea to the mountains and in between too,
Is a true testimony of what all God can do!
Every morning, I chose to begin in this way,
For this time of prayer, was a great start to my day.

We traveled by van, well loaded down
To help those that lived in a nearby town.
We saw many patients who were waiting there
Inside a small church which was nearly bare.
A few wooden tables and benches were just about all
That adorned the inside of this cement block hall.
As soon as we could, we unloaded our van
And set up a clinic…of sorts…as was planned.

The dentists started extracting teeth, full of decay,
And folks waited to see what the doctor would say.
Some of us sorted medicine and bagged lots of pills
To treat worms and infections and all sorts of ills.
The weather was so hot and humid in there....
We were soon all perspiring and wished for cool air.
Instead of glass windows, steel bars covered the spaces,
And often through these, we'd see inquisitive faces.

The people patiently waited...young, old, babies too...
The first day, rather anxious about what we might do.
The second day we were there, we saw many more.
They were friendly and eager, as they lined up by the door.
Some offered to help, others held a friend's hand
Who was still not quite sure, what all we had planned.
Now, they returned our smiles so much more
And most were less anxious than they had been before.

The poverty could easily be seen everywhere,
And it was apparent...they really needed our care.
As the week went on, the numbers increased,
And it was hard to leave when our work day ceased,
But we'd go back to the Inn where we stayed each night,
And the sea and good dinner were a most welcome sight.
Rice and beans are their staple and eaten each day,
Plantains were deep fried and were eaten that way.
Fish and other seafood were really so good
And we all ate more than we probably should.

We learned that the word had been spread far and wide,
In Santana and villages around this countryside.
We took useful items to the school that was there;
For it was apparent that they, too, needed our care.
The dirt roads were stony and rough as could be,
Cattle, pigs, and chickens roamed unfenced and free.
Not many had cars, so they walked or rode a bike…
Some rode in carts, horse drawn and the like.

Pineapples grew in the fields nearby
And as we flew in, palms were seen from the sky.
There were palm nut plantations from which palm oil is made,
And we ate small sweet bananas , at the place where we stayed.
We visited the Loma de Luz Hospital one day
And the "Sanctuary" Houses where families can stay.

How many aches and pains did we cure?
And how many were helped? … I'm really not sure,
But I do know that we all worked very hard
To ease pain and show love in this regard.
They came every day, dressed in the best that they had,
And saying "Good-bye" really made us all sad;
For we made new friends and felt their love too,
And the reward we received was tremendous, it's true.

Lord, help us continue to be your hands, heart, and feet
And let us show Your Love to all those whom we meet.

The Americas

There is so much to explore around this earth
That sometimes it's hard to decide,
Just where to go and about what to write
In a world with such vast countryside.
I'll try here to summarize briefly
Just a few of the places I've gone,
And tell of some things that there are to see,
From Alaska to the great Amazon.

The United States is a good place to start,
So let me begin this rhyme there.
Our National Parks (and I've been to most all)
Offer landscapes beyond compare:
There are mountains majestic and towering trees,
Huge glaciers and waterfalls high;
Endless deep canyons and seashores still wild,
Even deserts, so hot and dry.

Then one can go north or one can go south
And the variety continues to grow.
The Provinces of Canada have unique beauty too,
And they're much different than old Mexico.
The Panama Canal was an experience to cruise…
And one that I'll never forget,
Or the aerial tram through the tops of the trees
In a Rainforest that, of course, was quite wet.

Going on further south in the Americas
To the volcanoes in Ecuador,
And then off the coast, The Galapagos,
with rare creatures there by the score...
Things like the blue-footed booby, iguanas,
Penguins and huge tortoises too.
With no fear of humans, and they're all so unique;
It's much more fun than a zoo.

In Chile, the geoglyph marks in the desert,
And the Andes with glacial landscape.
How well I remember those "30 foot seas,"
When we sailed down 'round the Cape.
In Cusco I hiked among ancient ruins
And then the Inca trail in Peru...
What a thrill it was as the clouds disappeared
And Machu Picchu came into view.

Then from the world's southernmost city—
Ushuaia, Argentina—we flew
To Antarctica with ice, snow, and mountains,
And wind that constantly blew.
The Iguazu Falls near Paraguay...
So vast and a true delight,
And all the birds and butterflies there
Just enhanced that lovely sight.

Brazil has that mighty Amazon
With all the flooded rainforest too.
I'll never forget that dark, stormy night
when I went out in a dugout canoe
From an Indian village in the jungle
With a native that I didn't know
Who proceeded to catch a Cayman
And then bring it, to hold and to show.

I remember the eyes in the darkness
Every time the guide flashed his light
Which really made me wonder
Just what was there—hidden from sight.
We canoed under low-hanging branches
On trees that were submerged 30 feet,
And hearing those strange jungle sounds
Was really an interesting treat.

I could write pages about these adventures,
For they're such exciting places to see,
And I have not even mentioned so many,
Like New York City, Alaska or Hawaii.
There are museums, festivals and cultures,
Interesting people and so much more,
But I'll leave some things for another time,
For there's always much yet to explore.

Adventures in Iceland and Greenland

Greenland and Iceland are both interesting scenes,
But most of Greenland is ice and much of Iceland is green.
The Vikings first came to this place long ago,
And have remained here for 32 generations or so.
There are Icelandic horses, and a few sheep graze,
And in summer there are 22 hour-long days.
Now in winter, it's very windy, dark and cold,
But not really much snow, or so I've been told.
One third of the world's lava is located here,
But with the moss on that lava, often green will appear.
The moss makes an inch of soil, in 70 years or so,
And after 5000, there's enough for crops to grow.
Mud pots, hot springs and geysers abound,
With volcanic mountains and glaciers all around.
There's lots of hot water…it's the cheapest thing there.
When turning on the spigot, you must do it with care,
For the temperature when it comes from under the ground
Is an amazing 800 degrees, and there's steam all around.
It heats their homes, swimming pools and greenhouses too;
The air's very clean, but skies are more gray than blue.
There aren't many trees, and the ones there are low.
It's the fishing that allows their economy to grow.
The people are friendly, blond and tall,
And Icelandic and English are taught to all.
It's a country that is so interesting to see:
It's quite different and unique, I think you'd agree.

While I was in Iceland, I found out I could go
To Greenland, if there were nine, and not too much snow.
There happened to be eight others as eager as I
To have this adventure…so they said we could fly.
Two were from Scotland, five Germans…one from India too,
With our guide from Iceland, we made quite a crew!
It was the first trip of the year and as we boarded the plane,
There was sun in Iceland, but in Greenland it was all sleet and rain.
There were two young men also on the plane when we went,
Who had "rescue sleds" with them…we wondered what that meant.
We crossed the Arctic Circle, and as I looked down,
I could see snow-covered mountains and icebergs around.
We landed…not on tarmac, but gravel and mud,
And not a soft landing, but one that came with a thud!
Our guide had said on the plane before,
That we'd leave the "civilized world" when we walked out that door.
There would be no bathrooms and nothing to eat,
But that didn't matter…the "trip" was the treat.

We entered their airport…such as it was…
And were told we'd start hiking, with barely a pause,
But the road was so icy and the mud was so deep,
That our guide said he'd take us part way in a jeep.
The road got much worse and the snow was piled high,
So he could drive no further, no matter how hard he'd try.
The wind was howling when he stopped to say
"From here you'll need to walk…there's just no other way!
Go up the mountainside where there are rocks and less snow,"
And then he hiked on to the village to let them know,
That we were coming, if ever we got through that snow!
Now I was not dressed for winter, for when I left home,
I didn't know that to Greenland, I'd be able to roam.
There was not any trail to help us find our way,
So we just aimed for the distant village beside the bay.
Now the bay, it was slushy and had started to thaw,
So we wondered really if we'd get there at all!

But we trudged through the snow and slid over the rock,
And got to the village in spite of the tough walk.
The village was Kulusuk and was really quite small,
In fact, it had less than 300 Inuits, when you counted them all.
They spoke no English, except for a few,
But they were eager to show us what they could do.
One man showed his kayak, made from a seal he had killed.
He then showed how he could harpoon...indeed he was skilled.
A grandmother showed us their native dance,
And we learned of their customs, since we had the chance.
The ships bring supplies when the ice isn't here,
That's three months in the summer, so the shelves were quite bare
They live on fish, seal and polar bear the rest of the year.
For they can grow very little in the soil around here.
The weather got worse...the plane had to leave while it could,
And with that weather, the walk would take more time than it should.
So they said, "We can take you part way by dogsled."
Now the dogs were all howling...They knew what was ahead.
We jumped on their crude sleds, and away we all flew,
Over the bay that was slush, and the sleet and wind blew!
With ice freezing on our glasses and the wind howling about
Suddenly the dogs stopped...and we had to get out!
The rocks on the mountainside just made it too rough
For these dogs to go further, even though they were tough.
So once again, we had no choice, if we wanted to go
So we all hurried back through the wind, sleet and snow!
What an adventure it was to see this remote place
And meet those so different in culture and race.
This world is so interesting and so very diverse;
I could write endlessly, but you'd be tired of the verse.
Just remember there's lots out there to enjoy and explore.
There are adventures everywhere...even outside of your own door

Adventures in Africa

In September of the year 2005
I took this trip that I'll now describe—
To Botswana, Namibia and Zimbabwe too;
Then on to South Africa before I was through.
It was in Johannesburg that I met our guide,
And off we went exploring the vast countryside.
The flight to get there was long, that's true,
But once I arrived—what spectacular views!

Over One thousand species of birds dwell there,
In all sizes, shapes and colors—some really rare.
One came in our cabin, as we went to bed,
"It's a red-billed wood hoopoe" or so the guide said,
Harmless, but very large, as it flew all about
And tried to decide just how to get out.
We often saw ostrich and fish eagles too
Vultures, hornbills and rollers, to name just a few.

All kinds of antelopes crossed our path,
As well as Cape buffalo, zebras, baboons and giraffes.
Roan antelope and sable, waterbuck and more,
Wildebeests, lechwe and impalas by the score—
Hippos and lions were all there to see,
Many elephants with babies—such diversity.
Termite mounds that were huge, were seen everywhere,
And at night we enjoyed watching the little springhare.

There were many snakes, and very poisonous too,
But only one ever came into my view.
I did have a scorpion in my journal one night,
But that encounter ended without too much fright.
There were not only sights but also sounds, often strange—
The roar of the lions within very close range—
The chime of the bell frogs on the Delta at night
While hippos grazed tent side in the full moon light.

In open vehicles we went on our daily 'game run'
Or in boats or small planes to get to the next one.
Oh, yes, it was usually dusty, bumpy, and hot,
But all that was worth it—for the views that I got.
There were all kinds of animals, birds and terrain,
And I was always eager and ready to go out again.
They'd wake us at 5:30 to the beat of the drum.
How exciting it was that a new day had begun.

We visited schools with children eager to tell
What they learned and they asked us questions as well.
We went to see villages and hear of their ways
And ate dinner with them on some of the days.
Some foods there were quite different, but I didn't mind,
And I found most of the people to be gracious and kind.
We were a small group of travelers, and none that I knew,
But all were so interesting and the friendships soon grew.

It was apparent that most of these Africans didn't have much
But were resourceful and creative with woodcarving and such.
They make 'termite cement' for huts roofed with thatch,
And weave straw into baskets and plates to match.
These countries have problems, of course, that's true
Lots of unemployment and AIDS—to list just a few.
In Soweto alone, three thousand funerals a week,
Yet with these problems and poverty, the birth rate's at its peak.

We often watched the sun slowly sink in the sky
In the Kalahari—with wild creatures really close by.
Or sometimes on the river, by a waterhole--- wherever we'd be—
There were always interesting sights there to see.
We heard the "rumble" of elephants and their "trumpeting" too—
The "squabbles" among baboons and the birds' constant "ca-coo."
Sometimes we'd have lunch "in the bush," under a tree,
And other days we'd stop to have a cup of "bush tea."

There were campfires and discussions and lectures too
About culture and history and what these folks do.
It was hard to believe that a wife could be bought,
And for just six cows each—four wives might be sought.
These African women must serve men and then sit on the floor,
They have lots of children and do so much more—
They carry water and cook—often can't go to school,
And in any decision—the men always rule.

We went next to Victoria Falls—a Natural Wonder, it's true.
We saw mongoose and monkeys, for they live there too,
But there were no warthogs, as we'd seen days before;
Instead, here were rainbows, mist and a thunderous roar.
The foliage here was like jungle—all green and dense,
But with all of the mist, that really made sense.
We had such informative guides along the way,
That increased our understanding of what we saw each day.

It was springtime then when I got to the Cape,
We still had blue skies, but now a "flowered" landscape.
Quite a contrast, indeed, from the hot desert sand,
To a cooler, green and mountainous land.
Now whales and penguins came into view
And the Ocean and Vineyards were visible too.
I hiked on the mountaintop and at the Cape of Good Hope—
Went to gardens and museums—what a kaleidoscope!

In traveling all seven continents and a hundred countries too,
　　I find many exciting things in this world to do.
　Adventures are just waiting to be discovered as well—
　　New people and cultures with their own stories to tell.
　Beautiful sights to see and places about which I've read,
　　It's like an open book with many experiences ahead.
　The memories of this trip will be filed with the rest,
　　All of them great--and the next always best.

　There were so many experiences that it's hard to tell
　　All these things in a poem—and do it all well.
　　But I hope I've inspired you to travel and see
　What an interesting place this world really can be.

Rivers of Thought

I sometimes think of Rivers and all the stories they could tell;
And lots of other waterways that I've traveled on as well…
Like going up the Amazon, 1000 miles or more,
Or cruising that Eternal Nile… viewing life along its shore.

Then there's the great Ganges in India, which is a religious space;
With funeral fires, people bathing and candles floating everyplace.
The castles along the Danube must have seen much more than war,
And that Canal that runs through Panama carries barges by the score.

Sometimes the Rivers tumble over falls so very high,
Like Victoria or Niagara, making rainbows in the sky.
And sometimes they are frozen and glaciers too are formed
Which then break off as icebergs at the edge where they are warmed.

Some Rivers are so peaceful as they slowly travel by,
But others may cause havoc when they flood with water high.
Many end up in the Oceans, as they wind along their way.
What a blessing all this water provides for us each day.

In some Rivers, clothes are washed and people meet along the edge,
And sometimes there may be a need for a channel to be dredged
For crops to grow or perhaps to lead to another waterway as well.
Just think of all the stories that these Rivers then could tell.

Travels in Europe

The first trip we made across the Sea
Was to Switzerland…what a beautiful country.
We'd been in all "48 States" on trips before,
So next the whole world was there to explore.
We went to Alaska and Hawaii too,
Before continuing on a more worldly venue.

Then to Ireland and Scotland and even Great Britain;
Vienna in Austria, where the Strauss Waltzes were written.
We saw Cathedrals and Castles and much history,
And around every turn….a new discovery.
Beautiful gardens in England, like Hampton Court and Kew;
Bagpipes in Scotland …Irish Pub Singing too.

Then the Netherlands and Russia and Poland as well,
With windmills, museums, and boat rides on the canal.
I can't forget Greece or Italy with ancient ruins to see
Or April in Paris…but that's another story.
Norway and Sweden have such picturesque coastlines,
And in Germany….steep vineyards, along the Rhine.

There are so many places on the Mediterranean too…
Quaint fishing villages and Greek Isles…(more than a few).
Monaco and The French Riviera are there as well,
And Portugal and Spain, with yet a different tale to tell.

I've not even mentioned Belgium and so many more,
And it's not that they're countries that I'd like to ignore;
For there's a special uniqueness in each place that I've been,
And to many of them, I've gone back again.
Each time I'm there I find something new,
And that's just another reason to keep traveling too.

Travels in India and Nepal

India, indeed, is a country of contrasts,
From the Taj Mahal to the beggars you pass.
Camels and carts amid buses and cars,
Rickshaws and bicycles, turbans and scarves.

Cows in the street, amid goats and trash,
And then the scene changes…just in a flash.
The smell is unique…cow patties and curry!
Aside from the traffic, no one seems to hurry.

It's a sensory overload, it seems to me,
And it makes me wonder, "How can this be?"
Elephants and mahouts, then monkeys appear.
There are forts and castles, stupas and deer.

From searching for tigers to cremations and more,
Every turn of the corner, a surprise was in store.
More food was served than we could possibly eat,
Yet, outside there were many who starved in the street.

It was amazing to see how they carried huge loads,
On their heads or on bicycles, on such chaotic roads.
The women were always in such colorful dress
Even when in the fields or in the midst of a mess.

The children were dear, although dirty and poor,
So easy to love…so hard to ignore.
"Hello, Madame," they all seemed to say,
As they persistently sold their wares every day.

Electricity goes off part of the time,
The water's polluted; the ponds covered with slime.
Rough roads are narrow, no guard rail or light,
As village and farmland pass out of sight.

Nepal is also an interesting spot,
With high Himalayas and terraced farm plots.
The people are happy and pleasant, it seems,
Whether carrying huge loads or washing in streams.

Incense and bells and gods by the score;
Hindu and Buddhist, Muslim and more.
Prayer wheels and flags, temples and shrines;
Chanting and praying…sometimes in rhymes.

Even when clouds hid Mt Everest from sight,
Still the beauty was an overwhelming delight.
We visited bazaars, homes, and schools too,
Museums and palaces, to name just a few.

We traveled by train, by bus, plane and cart,
A boat on the Ganges, a jeep in the park,
A rickshaw, a canter, and on elephant back,
By camel safari and a mountain "trek."

There was shopping and photos and so much to do;
Even the "rest stops" were an adventure, it's true.
A hole in the floor or perhaps just in the ground
Seemed better than when only a bush could be found.

More could be written about how exciting a view,
To see the wild tigers and snake charmers too.
And that Taj Mahal…what an awesome sight,
As its marble and jewels caught the first morning light.

What an interesting culture and country to see,
And I remember how gracious they were to me.
We all have so much, and so little have they.
Yes, indeed, we are blessed to live in the U.S.A.

Bucharest to Prague and So Much More

This trip started in Bucharest and Constanta then came
With a two-hour ride on our own private train.
Then we boarded the ship, "Aria," by name
And began the cruise—one of the reasons we came.

From Romania to Bulgaria, on the Black Sea and Canal,
Then on to the Danube and new adventures as well.
We all had a color: Blue, Red, Yellow and Green,
And often took bus rides, so the countryside could be seen.

We enjoyed "home-visits" with good food—often too much;
It was nice to meet people, learn their culture and such.
We saw ancient churches and houses stacked on a hill,
And heard beautiful music, that was really a thrill!

Then on to the Iron Gates, through Locks one and two,
And suddenly steep mountains came into view.
There were Castles and Forts along the way,
Villages and farmland , and dogs that were stray.

We arrived in Serbia—had a tour of Belgrad,
And from there we sailed on to Nova Sad.
From Nova Sad to Croatia, we traveled some more
With great guides who told us about what was in store.

There were dancers and folk music and museums with art,
Lectures and shopping—even donkeys with cart.
Along the way we also had times for fun,
Being entertained by the crew was certainly one.

The people of Croatia were as gracious as could be;
But all the destruction and bullet holes were sad to see.
To hear tales of their life in the Communist days
And see how resilient they are, leaves nothing but praise.

In Budapest, we had rain most every day,
But our adventures weren't dampened in any way.
That gorgeous Opera House was a true delight,
Especially the concert surprise and the city view at night!

We crossed into Slovakia on our extension to Prague,
And again there was drizzle and even some fog.
But soon the sun came as we walked all about,
In a truly beautiful city, without a doubt!

I've made new friends and learned lots as well,
I have happy memories and new adventures to tell.
It was a great trip! As trips always are;
For each place is unique—whether near or far.
Travel makes me appreciate what I have back home,
But also inspires me to continue to roam.

Travels in the Far East

This trip to the Orient, began in Beijing,
Where I climbed the Great Wall—what a memorable thing!
It was steeper and wider than I thought it would be,
And for miles across mountain tops, it was easy to see.
Sometimes there were ramps, then uneven steps might appear,
With openings for guards to see when the enemy came near.

Strong winds blew at the Wall & on the ground there was snow!
Hard to imagine just how high the temperatures later would go.
The Forbidden City, Peking Opera, and Tiananmen Square,
Were also a part of the interesting sights there.
Beijing is hosting the Olympics in 2008,
They're busy building and renovating for that special date.

Then on to the coast...I boarded the ship for the cruise,
Where I'd sail many days for more exciting venues!
Two devastating typhoons were here days before,
Which caused one to wonder just what might be in store,
But the weather was great for this time of year—
Cold in the north...hot as the equator drew near.

In fact, as I sat looking over the East China Sea,
I marveled at how peaceful and calm it could be.
Folks from 69 countries were aboard this ship--
Interesting people...made a more interesting trip!
I traveled to 7 countries and 10 ports-of-call—
Flew 14,000 miles and sailed 5000 in all.

Of course, there were many side trips, as well,
By boat, bus or rickshaw--with an adventure to tell—
Like when the small boat capsized on Lake Chini one day,
Near a primitive village where they spoke only "Malay."
The Asian toilets were also an adventure, it's true—
Just a hole in the floor and never any tissue!
Asian food was usually spicy hot, always with rice,
And dessert, other than watermelon, would have been nice.

After China, Korea was where I next stepped ashore,
And there found another culture to explore.
The currency in Korea was nearly 1000 to our 1.
Cost of living was high…all inheritance goes to the son.
Korea is divided, of course, as you know,
And folks from the South to the North cannot go.

Then on to Japan, with many volcanoes, it's true—
I visited a city that had been buried from view.
Here we drove to the countryside and saw how life used to be,
And a "Big Drum" performance was exciting to see!
Leaves were in color on this perfect fall day,
And I saw them harvesting sea weed along the bay.

Next came Shanghai…with Temples and Buddhas by the score.
I visited a school, a museum, beautiful gardens and more.
In Asia most are Buddhists or Hindu, with some Muslim too—
Lots of Monks and incense burning…there are many rituals they do.
They have superstitions about numbers, colors, and all sorts of things—
Laws prohibit cats and dogs, but you can have a bird that sings.

They take their bird walking and they do Tai Chi,
There's only one child permitted for each family.
There are police everywhere in this Chinese city,
And one realizes how precious freedom can be.
An acrobatic show was hard to believe—
So agile and flexible—amazing what they can achieve.

In Hong Kong, Lantau Island was unique and quite old,
And sea creatures of all shapes and sizes were sold.
These folks live in quaint houses, built on stilts in the sea—
Quite a contrast from Hong Kong—I found this to be.
Hong Kong orchids grow everywhere and skyscrapers 80 floors high,
Full of 300 square foot apartments to rent--not buy.
Then from Hong Kong we sailed on a December night,
From a harbor aglow with bright Christmas light.

In Vietnam—water buffalo and rice paddies abound—
Thousands of mopeds and bicycles—shelled corn dried on the ground.
The Open Market was busy and one couldn't ignore—
All the fly-covered meats…seen nowhere before.
Then I visited a farm to see where they dwell,
And watched them make rice paper and rice noodles as well.

Roads often were muddy and littered, that's true:
But people smile and are friendly—vendors like bargaining with you.
Vietnam is mountainous and lush and green,
And all the fruits and coconuts, make a delicious cuisine.
In Saigon, a uniform must be worn by each one,
This designates which school or where your work is done.

In Thailand, the elephants were amazing and smart—
　As they played soccer and danced and even did art!
You could tell they enjoyed it, by their response to the crowd,
And as they mingled with people, they were gentle and proud.
Thai dancers, boxers, and warriors showed their talents as well,
Through their performance and music, their heritage they'd tell.

　In Malaysia, the jungle trip was a highlight for me—
　　With monkeys and birds and huge towering trees.
　　Some trees reaching more than 300 feet high,
　With dense foliage and vines, one could barely see sky!
　　Rubber plantations and palms were seen here too,
　And bamboo blowguns are used for the hunting they do.
In Malaysia, the monkeys harvest coconuts from the tree,
But as in most of these countries, people aren't really free.

　In Singapore, it's hot and humid, but so lush and green;
　　It's quite a contrast to see things so sterile and clean.
Beautiful flowers, skyscrapers, and a mix of cultures, it's true;
　　But lots of plain clothes police watch what you do.
　　There are no guns or drugs or littering here,
　　And a long list of rules with punishments severe.
　　I took a trip to see orchids and to a nice zoo,
　　Even a "Singapore Sling" and a trishaw ride too.

The ship quarantine flags are—yellow, orange, and red...
Depending on how many are 'sick and in bed'.
We had about 700, I heard them say..
Nearly 30% of the passengers were in 'sick bay'.
They were quarantined in their cabins, thankfully the ship could go on
Into each port-of call, though the flu wasn't quite gone.

I went to lectures and stage shows when on the ship too,
These were very informative and fun things to do.
Yes, it was another GREAT trip (perhaps I say that every time)
I have many great memories, more than I can put in a rhyme.
There were different cultures and people and always a new sight
But that's what makes traveling such a delight.

Australia, New Zealand and the South Pacific

What a thrill to go snorkeling on the Great Barrier Reef.
The fish, coral, and sea creatures are beyond belief.
With colors, and shapes, and numbers beyond measure;
It was an awesome experience that I'll always treasure.

The Aboriginal art and culture are interesting too,
Cave paintings and music played on the derigadoo.
Of course, the Opera House in Sydney is a "must see,"
And the harbor around there is really quite lovely.

Lots of opals are mined inland where it's hot and dry.
Quite a contrast from the Reef with the rainforest nearby.
From Australia, to both islands of New Zealand , I flew,
Took a train up the Mountain, visited a sheep ranch there too.

New Zealand is quite different in a great many ways
With more sheep than people, also hot springs and caves.
Australia has the Blue Mountains, but they're not nearly as high
As the New Zealand Alps that seem to reach to the sky.

It's the only place in the world where the "glow worms" are found
Deep in dark caves; they "glow" only when there's not a sound.
There are lots of other creatures unique to these countries too
Like the kiwi, the platypus, koala and kangaroo.

From Australia and New Zealand, on to Fiji, on the way home,
An island country with 300 islands on which one can roam;
Lush palms and beaches and tropical flowers abound,
Similar to many other South Pacific Islands around.

Life seems to move at a slower pace there.
No one gets excited or seems to worry or care.
Isn't it interesting how different all these places can be?
That's why it's such fun to explore them and see.

Travel Souvenirs

The memories of places traveled
Fill my mind with pleasure.
Of the time and place, the sights and sounds;
All these and more, I treasure.

The word "souvenir" means "to remember,"
And I have found this to be true,
That a fun way to relive those times
Is with a souvenir or two.
For when I look at some I have,
The memories flood my mind,
Of sights I've seen and people met…
Experiences of every kind.

Souvenirs can be anything
That is significant to you;
Perhaps a book, a postcard,
Or a photograph or two.
Sometimes the challenge is to find
Things small enough to pack;
And also things that make nice gifts
To give when you get back.

I collect small boxes
That remind me of a place.
And local music instruments
If I can find the space.
I like to meet the person
Who has made a craft to sell;
For then it means much more,
When their story they will tell.

But the best part is not the souvenir,
Even though that is great fun…
It's meeting people, seeing places,
And doing things, you've never done.

"Westward Ho, the Wagons"
The Majestic U.S. National Parks

This trip began in South Dakota…Rapid City was the place,
A town with statues of Presidents on every corner space.
There were 44 of us, traveling on this journey west,
With a guide and driver that really were the best!
We made discoveries, quite interesting, and we learned so much
About History, Geology, Indians, Pioneers, and such.
We were from various parts of the U.S., and quite different, it's true,
But we soon became friends that enjoyed each new view.

Crazy Horse and Mt. Rushmore were the first sights that we'd see,
And that night program at Rushmore, really impressed me.
The Black Hills, the Plains, then Devils Tower rose up high;
And when we hiked 'round the base, there was a sunny blue sky.
We crossed the Big Horn Mountains, in the midst of a snowfall.
Then on to "Dirty Annie's" and "Cowboy Irv," with horse and all.
There were lush green valleys, ranches and even prairie dogs to see
In Wyoming, where many cattle still roam free.
The Bill Cody Museum was an interesting place,
And wild horses were seen in Wyoming's wide open space.

It was then in Yellowstone when I injured my knee
That I learned just how kind my fellow travelers could be.
We stayed in this park and "Old Faithful" erupted right on time;
There were mud pots and hot springs…all the views were sublime.
Waterfalls, canyons, and lakes …among mountains so high.
We saw wolves, deer, and elk…but no bear ever passed by.
The buffalo were many and not hard to see;
We even had a picnic there, underneath a pine tree.

The majestic Tetons rise right up from the Lake,
With their Glaciers and sharp peaks…what a picture they make!
Arches of Elk Horns, graced Jackson's town square
Old buildings and wood sidewalks..like the "Old West" was still there.
We visited an artist whose home was different indeed,
And floated down the Snake River at a nice easy speed.
"Seven Brides for Seven Brothers" was a play we saw there,
And the music and acting were beyond compare.
There was a little log Chapel that has a divine view,
For through the large altar window, the Tetons show through.

In Salt Lake City, the Mormons graciously showed us around,
And we listened to their choir…What a heavenly sound!
The Tabernacle and Museum and Temple Square
Had beautiful flowers blooming everywhere.
A side trip to Park City was interesting too,
To see where Winter Olympics were held in 2002.

Then came Bryce Canyon with those beautiful "Hoodoos,"
And Sunrise and Sunset provided even different views.
Cove Fort was our "Discovery Surprise" one day
And it proved worth the effort to go out of our way.
The Vermillion Cliffs and where the Colorado River began;
Also National Forests and Canyons were in our travel plan.

The North Rim of the Grand Canyon, I can't forget that,
With its awesome panorama and wind that blew off your hat!
That boat ride on Lake Powell had unforgettable sights,
With water so blue and huge rocks…a photographer's delight!
There were deserts with mesas, buttes and occasionally a creek
And the Slot Canyons with sandstone shapes so unique.
It was so windy at the "Slots" that we had sand everywhere,
And actually quite an adventure, just to get there….
On the back of a truck, down a riverbed dry…
But the colors and shapes…what a treat for the eye!

Wildflowers bloomed brightly along the way,
And God blessed us with sunshine most every day.
It was wonderful to see wildlife in their natural home
Out here, in the West, where the buffalo once roamed.
There were pronghorns, wild turkeys, fox, moose, and mule deer.
Around every turn, something new would appear.
Osprey and eagles, loons and white pelicans too,
Yellow-headed blackbirds and goshawks, to name just a few.
All kinds of trees that were different as well,
Like bristle cone pine and too many others to tell.
Coal and copper mines, ranches, and cowboys too
And always a gift hhop and shopping to do!

In Navajo Country…Hogans, sagebrush and not much more,
'Till Monument Valley sprung up from that desert floor.
Those Monoliths were certainly a sight to behold…
The perfect backdrop for movies…or so I've been told.
In Durango, the Hotel was beside a nice stream,
With balconies and cookies, it was a "Traveler's Dream."
The Cliff Dwellers at Mesa Verde…What can I say?
It's hard to imagine how they built in this way.
So long ago without tools as an aid,
They created buildings that through centuries have stayed.

Next, we boarded that Train for Silverton, up high,
And there were "Kodak Moments" every place we passed by.
That bear that we wanted so badly to see,
Suddenly appeared…climbing a tree.
Then that incredible drive over the Million Dollar Highway
With more spectacular views than I really can say.

Sometimes we watched videos or Judy gave us a "test,"
We really tried hard to get the prize for the "best;"
And a postcard was usually the only reward we received
For all that "brain power" we had to use to achieve.
We'll never forget her little clock, for the time…
It did, at least, help keep us a little bit "in line."
While Richie kept struggling as our luggage gained weight,
His smile never ceased, and his driving was "first rate."
Now Judy was great and told us about each new sight;
Her only problem was knowing her left from her right.
A guide and a driver can make or break a trip, that's true…
Richie and Judy this trip was "The Best," thanks to you!

So now, it's on back to Denver, and we'll all go our own ways,
With WONDERFUL MEMORIES of 17 FANTASTIC DAYS!

The Land of the Midnight Sun

This poem begins in Finland, for that's where we all met,
To journey through two countries, on a trip I'll not forget.
We were 44 eager travelers—there was none I'd known before;
But soon the friendships started, as we began our tour.

It was quite warm in Helsinki, much warmer than we thought,
And we didn't need the warm clothes that most of us had brought.
The skies were bright and sunny, as we ventured all around
To learn, see, and discover, what new things could be found.

The Memorial to Sibelius and Olympic Park from '52,
The Town Square and Cathedral—Yes, the sights were quite a few.
The Crafts and Produce at the Market Place and also the old Fort,
The boat ride and the Harbor—It was an interesting port.

When we crossed the Arctic Circle and arrived at Ivalo,
The countryside was different, and the temperature was also.
It was there we first met Sami and had some reindeer stew.
We learned about their way of life and what it is they do.

No, the Northern Lights, we didn't see—not at this time of year;
But when we got to Lapland, lots of reindeer did appear.
We met a herder's family—we were their special guests;
They talked about their culture, and the meaning of their dress.

We hiked along a ski trail—tasted Finnish sausage too,
Learned about Black Fungus and how crow berries grew.
Fresh Salmon and cloud berries were quite a treat one day
When we ate inside a Teepee, along our Northern way.

This land of Lakes and Forests, had so many hours of light,
Of course, then in the winter, it's just one long, dark night.
We stopped to see a Russian Church and cemetery too;
The graves were topped with Reindeer Moss—this is where it grew.

We learned about the history of wars and so much more;
Visited museums and lots of places that we had never been before.
One day we had a coffee break—that surprise was really neat,
Beside a lake they built a fire, and coffee vodka was the treat!

We left Finland then & traveled north, toward Norway & Russia too.
The "Cold War" may be over, but Russia still watches what you do.
From Finland into Norway—we crossed in just no time;
But the soldier with his dog came out, at the Russia borderline.

Then to the ship to travel south, out in the Barents Sea,
Along fjords, the ports-of-call totaled 33,
We stopped at little villages and islands by the score,
To pick up cars and cargo—even people and much more.

There were brightly painted houses at these ports-of-call,
And so many interesting sights, I cannot name them all.
The scenes were always changing, and ships were passing by;
The weather here was cool and rainy and sometimes no blue sky.

The weather didn't stop us from having a good time.
We went ashore and walked about, the adventures were sublime!
All were quite compatible, and Matt, our guide, was great.
The ship was nice, the food was good—lots to appreciate.

The mountains were majestic---some had glaciers tucked up high;
And sunsets—Oh, so beautiful, as they lingered in the sky.
No poem can do them justice—no photograph can tell
The beauty of those mountains, and how vast they are as well.

When we went into the Troll Fjord, we could almost touch rock walls;
And in between some rocks, there were tumbling waterfalls.
Some mountainsides were green and lush & some were really bare,
In some places there were wild flowers—blooming everywhere.

I've eaten lots of different things, as I've traveled far and wide;
But I had never tasted whale until I reached this countryside.
We ate moose and cheese and berries, and yes, all kinds of fish—
And that's all part of travel—trying each new dish.

We learned about the Vikings, and we did some shopping too.
We shared our travel stories, the way all travelers do.
Most took a lot of photos, to remember, when back home,
And to add to that collection, of other places we may roam.

The sky was always changing, clouds drifted to and fro;
One minute there'd be sunshine—then rain and wind would blow.
The sea was mostly calm, though some white caps did appear.
The water here was very deep and never very clear.

Then when we got to Bergen, we bid our ship adieu,
And found our luggage heavier and our bodies heavier too.
Bergen was a unique old city by the bay,
Where rain is the usual, most every day.

Quaint tilted shops, stacked by the street,
And little fishing villages, made the scene complete.
Wild sheep roamed among the rock and pine,
Heather covered hillsides, in a picturesque design.

From Bergen, then to Oslo, we went by bus and train—
Mountains high, with waterfalls, such beautiful terrain!
A boat ride in a foggy mist and lots of tunnels too;
Stories of those little trolls and all the things they do.

Stave churches, grass-roofed cottages, and dinner by a lake,
Then in Oslo, sculpture gardens and museums, to appreciate.
From Oslo to Helsinki, and we're on our way back home,
To unpack and then to think where next we might roam.

Yes, the world's full of adventures—just look around,
With every journey, there are new things to be found.

Bon Voyage!

So Many Ways to Travel

Sometimes when I travel, the excitement and the fun,
Is in the means of getting to the trip that I've begun.

It may be in a taxi or a crowded subway train,
Or perhaps it's in a rickshaw or a jeep through rough terrain.

I've often thought when I have walked over trails of long ago,
If those historic paths could talk…what stories they would know.

I've hiked deep in the jungles…seen treetops from a tram,
Been on ski lifts and gondolas…canal boats in Amsterdam.

In sleighs drawn by horses and sleds pulled by dogs,
On trains through the mountains and in canoes made from logs.

I've gone in submarines and kayaks…flown in helicopters too,
Ridden camels when in India, and hiked on trails in Peru.

Took balloon rides over Africa, also parasailed up high,
Went snorkeling in Australia and flew in planes high in the sky.

Been on sailboats and cruise ships and hover crafts so fast:
Also trekked the Himalayas and rode elephants….what contrast.

Whether cruising down a river, riding in a bus or a streetcar,
It's really quite amazing, how many ways to travel that there are.

The Canadian Rockies

Some people say they don't like snow, and I often wonder why,
For it gently paints such beauty, as it falls down from the sky.
To see snow lay upon the trees and dress the pines in white
And freeze on waterfalls and creeks is such a lovely sight.

It was in this wintertime, that I saw the Rockies at their best…
The mountains with their majesty, frozen lakes and all the rest.
A train ride through the countryside, indeed, was a delight,
As was the sleigh ride on Lake Louise, as snow fell, fresh and light.

Around every bend was a surprise in this unique landscape,
And Santa even came aboard at a stop the train did make.
The wildlife was impressive, as they foraged for some grass…
Bighorn sheep, mule deer and elk were seen while in the train we passed.

I had seen this mountain country in the summer years ago,
And had often longed to see these sights when covered white with snow.
There was no disappointment, for the beauty was still there
But now with more icicles and snowdrifts everywhere.

Polar Bears and So Much More

This poem's about a trip I took to Churchill, on the Bay,
When I went to see the Polar Bears, one October day.
There were many Arctic creatures, on that Tundra by the shore.
It was a great adventure, to see the bears and so much more!

There are no roads into the town…Churchill is the name;
So in a plane from Winnipeg was the way by which we came.
Once we left this little town, our feet never touched the ground;
Because we could have been a treat for the hungry bears around.

It was in a Tundra Buggy where we would spend each day;
And at night, the Buggy Lodge was the place that we would stay.
Here we only had a bunk, and, yes, the space was small,
But we could spend nights on the Tundra, so we didn't mind at all.

The bears appeared outside the Lodge, when they smelled our dinner cook,
And there was much excitement, as we ate and had a look.
For lunch we always ate where we could check activity,
And even though it's desolate, there was always much to see.

The Tundra Trails were rough and rocky; yes, travel there was slow,
And often there were tundra ponds through which we had to go.
The Buggy really was built high with tires five feet or so;
For bears can have a 12-foot reach and shatter windows with one blow.

There had been some snow two days before; but now none could be seen.
Our days were mostly clear, with cold and cloudy in between.
Not many trees will grow there, only spruce, and they're quite small.
With the windy, cold, dark winters, I wondered how they grew at all.

There are willow shrubs among the rocks, and mosses are there too.
The shades of brown and red and gold, add color to the view.
The willow buds were tufts of white and almost looked like snow,
And in among them, ptarmigans would scamper to and fro.

We watched a snow white Arctic fox as he caught and ate his prey
And an Arctic hare was also on the Tundra that same day.
There were also ducks and many birds and even caribou,
Of course, the Polar Bears were mainly what we came to view.

And, yes, we did see many…and what a thrill to see!
That largest carnivore on earth looked as gentle as could be.
As they patiently waited for their icy hunt to start
We noticed they were curious and also seemed quite smart.

The Polar bears spend summer, without much food at all;
Then they come here, just to wait for the ice to freeze each fall.
And when it does, they then can go out on the Bay at last,
To wait close by a seal hole and catch one….if they're fast!

A real bonus on this trip was in the middle of the night,
When the Aurora Borealis suddenly appeared so bright.
As colors danced across the sky in shades of pink and green,
It was one of the most awesome sights that I had ever seen!

Our group came from 'round the world, with a common goal in mind,
There were none that I had known before; but as I often find,
That's really not a problem, for travelers mingle well,
And most have a travel story that they will freely tell.

One day we watched a "Bear lift"… that's used when some bears
go astray,
And venture into town where they find people in their way.
These bears then are tranquilized and in a net they fly
To places that are more remote where people aren't close by.

Some people, I'm sure, must wonder why would someone want to go,
To a place that's cold and desolate, where nothing much will grow,
To not even have a nice hotel or comforts like at home;
But there are always unique sights wherever you may roam.

The Middle East

On this Middle East adventure, it was in '97 that I went
To visit some dear friends, and there two weeks I spent.
The hospitality of these friends and others that I met
And the kindness that they showed me are things I'll not forget.
Syria was where I stayed….not a place where many travelers go,
And many customs there, are unlike the culture that we know.
Most folks there are Muslim and there were five daily "Calls to Pray."
From the many minarets, loud "Calls" came early every day.

Where I stayed was in Damascus, for most of this time;
Then I traveled east and north and south, to the borderline.
Damascus is the world's oldest populated city, so they say.
And 'Silk Road' traders long ago, always passed this way.
To cross a country's border is more complicated here.
And everywhere the statues and huge posters make it clear
That this country has a Dictator, who decides what all should do.
We were even stopped and asked just why we were there too.

Yes, it's a different culture with foods and customs quite unique;
The people there are friendly, but not much English do they speak.
Family life and hospitality are important to their way,
And the market and the kitchen consume most of a woman's day.
Photographs are often not allowed, one must be careful too,
And not speak about the government or discuss what it is they do.
One young man apologized when a photo was denied,
"Sorry, they're so strict," he said. "We're always afraid," he sighed.

I traveled through the desert, as sand blew everywhere,
To the ancient city of Palmyra and saw many ruins there.
I stopped and had a coffee with some Bedouins on the way…
Much stronger than the fresh mint tea that I'd had another day.
I bargained for some music instruments that they had made,
And then they even showed me, just how these things were played.
Carts and buses were overloaded…sheep and goats roamed free,
Some folks lived in mud domed huts; they were interesting to see.

To bargain in the market place was always fun to do.
To watch the craftsmen make their wares was amazing too.
I saw special places in the Christian part of town, as well,
Places mentioned in the Bible, about which the Scriptures tell.
Where Ananias healed Paul's sight…as the Lord told him to do.
And there are many other things, I've only mentioned just a few,
I hope I've written something, that you didn't already know,
And maybe even spoke of places, where you might want to go.

People and Places beyond the Familiar

I remember the Amazon and the jungle at night
In a dug-out canoe with only one flashlight.
It was so dark in the forest, and the rain poured down,
As thunder and lightning flashed all around.
Bright eyes glistened, as the guide flashed his light
In that flooded forest on that dark stormy night.

This guide spoke little English, as we floated about,
Then he suddenly stopped and in the water, got out.
As I sat with two fellow travelers whom I didn't know,
We pondered together why and where he would go,
For we knew that the water was 30 feet deep,
And all the night critters were not sound asleep.

We sat motionless…just listening for quite a long while,
Then he suddenly appeared with a big broad smile,
For he'd caught a live Cayman which he brought back to show.
Amazed! We all held it, and then let it go.
Catching a three-foot crocodile was hard to believe.
In this dark stormy jungle…What a feat to achieve!

We then began to wonder how he could find his way
Back to the village where we'd been that day.
It was there that we'd eaten…just what, we weren't sure.
Parrots came to eat from our plates and bits on the floor.
These natives were gracious and shared what they had
And though it was different, it didn't taste bad.

The children had pets, not like those that we knew:
They had monkeys, parrots, sloths…unfamiliar snakes too.
There are no roads in this jungle; travel is by boat here,
And to hike, our guide needed a machete to clear.
Yes, this was an adventure that was exciting and fun
And I'd recommend it, as a most interesting one.

By contrast, there's Rio with great beaches and all;
And on the mountain top, the Christ statue, 120 feet tall.
The sidewalks have mosaic patterns made from tiles
That are unique to each area and cover many miles.
Fiestas and carnivals are often held here.
This part of Brazil is not like the Amazon…that's very clear.

The Iguassu Falls are magnificent, and as I hiked all around,
I could hardly believe the beautiful butterflies I found.
There are 275 waterfalls with the mist rising high
And a thundering roar, even before you're nearby.
The view from a helicopter was quite an awesome sight,
And a boat trip near the base was another delight!

Then on down to the tip and around Cape Horn;
Here's where sailors often dread high seas and storm,
But the day we rounded, it was calm as could be;
However, next day there was a 30-foot sea…
And the waves splashed up, over seven decks high,
Along the Chilean coast, as the Andes passed by.

Ushuaia is the city on the South American tip,
And from here to Antarctica I went for a trip.
What an interesting continent of ice and snow,
With mountains and penguins and temperatures low.
So vast and white and windy and dry;
With huge icebergs in an Ocean as blue as the sky.

Then into the desert in Chile, where the ancient Geoglyphs remain
So large on the mountain side, they can be seen from a plane.
Who made them and why is a mystery today,
But perhaps for the Incas they were signs pointing the way.
To walk in this desert, which was so hot and dry
Was quite a contrast from snow-covered Andes nearby.

At Machu Picchu, it was a true traveler's highlight,
Seeing the clouds part and that Mountain come into sight.
It's an interesting trip from Cusco to these ruins in Peru…
On a train through the valley that the Incas all knew.
When we came back to Lima, there had been problems there,
And military and tanks were on the streets everywhere.
The U. S. President flew into Lima that day,
And we saw his plane land as our ship pulled away.

I took a photo in Ecuador with a volcano in the background
The next day it erupted, and there was ash all around.
Then we went to the Galapagos…wildlife had no human fear.
It's really special to see and particularly so near.
Blue footed Boobies, huge tortoises, iguanas, and more
Different species than I'd ever seen anywhere before.

To cross the Canal in Panama takes a whole day;
But it's so interesting that I didn't mind the delay.
For as the locks raise and lower, other ships come into view,
And they're from all over the world with cargo and crew.

There are so many islands and none seem quite the same;
The Galapagos, with the critters that are almost tame…
So different than Hawaii or Bermuda, it's true;
Or Iceland or the Greek Isles, to name just a few.
Most in the Caribbean are mountainous, lush and green
With beautiful flowers and colorful birds to be seen.
Of course, many have beaches and sunny hot weather too,
Which is great…until the hurricanes come through.

There are other adventures that now come to mind
Of other times and places…of a different kind.
In Egypt…the Pyramids and the Nile as well,
And what stories all those ancient sites could tell!
When I climbed the Pyramid, with an Egyptian guide,
It was very steep, dark, musty and hot inside.

The sites along the Nile were so unique too,
For these folks don't live the way we do.
It was as though time had really stood still there
And not many hurried or seemed to care.
The Valley of Kings and museums held so much…
Treasures, mummies, statues, and such.

Other countries in Africa are quite different, it's true,
With so many animals….like those seen in a zoo.
Except here they are native and all roam free,
And sometimes there are thousands…what a sight to see!
Over the Serengeti Plains, I floated in a hot air balloon…
Looking down on zebras, giraffes, wildebeests and baboon.

The sounds of migrating animals often fill the night air
Or the close roar of a lion can stir a bit of a scare.
On the Okavango Delta….What an awesome sight…
To have a hippo outside my tent one moonlight night.
While little bell-frogs sang and all else was so still:
Such sights and sounds always give me a thrill!

Sometimes a cape buffalo may stop and stare….
And that means…you better get out of there!
Elephants may tramp through the camp as well.
There really are so many tales to tell!
I could write also about all the people I've met,
With interesting cultures that I'll not forget.

Victoria Falls…what a treat…a beautiful sight,
The mist rises high, making rainbows so bright.
What a contrast it is from the desert nearby
Where, of course, it's always hot and dry.
Down by the Cape of Good Hope, there's Cape Town too,
And up on Table Top Mountain…what a fantastic view!

Australia and New Zealand are fun places to see.
The Great Barrier Reef has such diversity…
With coral and fish of every color and hue.
Also unique to this country are koala and kangaroo.
In the New Zealand caves, little worms hang down and glow
As long as you're quiet, they create quite a show.

The Far East, I've not mentioned yet, in this rhyme,
And the Great Wall of China was a real thrill to climb.
South Korea and Vietnam I found interesting as well;
Singapore and Thailand remind me of stories to tell.
I took a boat through the jungle in Malaysia one day,
To a village where natives spoke only "Malay."

India is really a sensory overload:
From the Taj Mahal to cows in the road.
Elephants to ride and tigers to see;
People worshiping and bathing in the Ganges.
The Himalayas in Nepal…spectacularly high
Snow covered peaks seem to reach to the sky.

Biblical places come alive, it's true,
At many sites in Israel and Syria too.
I remember the olive trees that remain to this day.
In Gethsemane's Garden, where Jesus prayed.
Visiting bazaars and Bedouins and having mint tea;
And floating was easy in the salty Dead Sea.

Scandinavian countries are crisp and clean,
With rocky coastlines and pines so green.
Russia has magnificent palace museums to see,
But otherwise, there seems to be much poverty.
Apartment buildings are grey and bare,
As though no one really seems to care.

Europe is the place that feels more like home.
And probably the most familiar of world places to roam.
There too, there's so much to see and do,
Castles , cathedrals, and historic places too.
To mention some of the countries, by name,
There's Ireland, England, Germany, Austria, and Spain,
Portugal, Switzerland, France, Italy, and Monaco,
The Netherlands, Belgium, Greece and even more, as you know.

Sometimes friends will ask which place traveled was best;
And if I try to pick one, it reminds me of the rest....
Of an adventure I had here or what I saw there,
The history, the beauty, the people...it's hard to compare.
Each place has an experience, just waiting to be found,
And that's why I've traveled this world all around....

There's so much to write about...so many places to go...
And I still think of much more that I'd like you to know
About this big wonderful world and all there is to see,
And what a blessing it is, to live in a country that's free.

All places and people are different....yes, that's true...
We have different customs and culture and things that we do;
But as I've traveled this world over, I really do find
That most people are friendly and usually quite kind.
And with traveling, perhaps we'll learn and understand;
How we can begin to live at peace in this land.

Bon Voyage!

Blessed to Be an American

How blessed we are in this country
That we can live where we are free!
Free to choose what work we'll do,
Free to speak and worship too.

Free from a Dictator's rule.
Free to learn and go to school.
And there are more that we could list
But still there would be some we'd miss.

And all this freedom is so nice,
But as we know, it has a price.
Some brave ones fought and gave their all;
Because they felt their country's call
To protect that freedom and keep the peace
Because it seems, wars never cease.

I often think Our Lord must cry
And shake His head and wonder why…
Why can't we all just live as brothers
Without the wars we have with others.

Around this world, we're much the same
Although we differ in race and name,
But as I travel the world, I find,
That really most folks are quite kind.
They work and love their family,
And would like to live in harmony.
They'd like to choose as we can here,
And live without the threats and fear.

Lord, help us to appreciate
Before it really is too late.
We know our country may have flaws
Within our democratic laws,
But show us how to do our best
To keep the freedoms we possess,
And still help others on their way
To live as free men every day.

About the Author

Born Elizabeth Jean Ritter, 'Betty' (as her family and friends know her) grew up on a farm in northwestern Pennsylvania. Having been married more than 54 years, she is the mother of 4 married children, the grandmother of 10 and the great grandmother of 2. As a retired Registered Nurse, Betty has had the pleasure of a lifetime of studying, teaching and playing music, as well. She has taught privately for 48 years and continues to teach piano in her home studio.

Betty began writing short rhymes for special occasions for her family several years ago. Poetry became more of a passion when she was asked to write for some events at her church in more recent years. Life situations and blessings continue to be an inspiration for her God-given talent. She has traveled extensively around the world, and the more exotic and adventurous the journey, the more exciting she finds it.

She continues to enjoy her home and family, teaching, traveling, painting, gardening, volunteering, reading, and of course, writing. Betty is an Elder, Clerk of Session and active member of Central College Presbyterian Church in Westerville, Ohio, where she and her husband now live.

ENDORSEMENTS

The Poet Laureate
of Central College Presbyterian Church

"There was never an event—either small or large, routine or tremendously significant—in the life of Central College Church which was not made more meaningful by a poem composed by Betty Meabon. She always had the ability to record in poetic form, not only the actual event but also the effect of that event upon the individuals involved. For those who were present and heard the reading of the poem there was a realization that they were part of a real life experience. For those who were not present but had the opportunity to read or hear the poem later, there was a true feeling of being connected with the people and activity of that particular event. This was a true blessing given to all of us through the gift of Betty Meabon and her poetic talent.

It was not always an event at the church which was captured and recorded by Betty. She has put life experiences into poetic form so that even a dull day becomes bright and beautiful by the touch of God through the words written by Betty. Her poems can lift the spirit, bringing sunshine into a rainy day. Her poems can also revive the spirit, bringing courage to the faint-hearted and comfort to the distraught. Her poems can put life into proper perspective and encourage individuals to look up from their everyday problems to the source of life, love and power. Her poems can mend the brokenheartedness of life and inspire individuals to move out of the shadows into the light of God's healing love. In short, the poems of Betty Meabon can—and do—put a perspective on life which makes the reader or hearer eager to walk with a new sense of purpose and joy.

I, for one, have been blessed to hear Betty read many of her poems. However, I know that this book of poems by my dear friend will be a source of inspiration for me, as I relive many of the experiences about which she has written, and as I permit her words of inspiration to penetrate my heart and mind, making life more significant in many meaningful ways. Betty Meabon is truly a blessing to all of us who have had the privilege of knowing her, and now she becomes a blessing to all who will read these poems and be renewed in spirit and mind."

Reverend Dr. Richard D. Ellsworth
Pastor Emeritus
Central College Presbyterian Church

"1 Peter 4:10 says, 'Each one should use whatever gift they have received to serve others, faithfully administering God's grace in its various forms.' In the 27 years I have known Betty she has used her gift of poetry to serve and inspire others as well as anyone I have ever known. Her willingness to share this book with all of us is a continuing example of this. It will inspire you."

Dave Cooper

"The Central College Presbyterian Church family is ecstatic that Betty Meabon has finally decided to share her poetry with a much larger audience. Betty's poems have deeply touched the hearts and minds of all who have been privileged to read or hear these beautifully, sensitively written poems of both secular and spiritual love. All her poetry, whether secular or religious, has a way of reaching the depths of our hearts and elicits a variety of emotions. As a friend of Betty and one who has been deeply moved by her poetry, I encourage everyone to take advantage of this literary opportunity, and you, too, will experience the joy of Betty Meabon's beautiful poetry."

Ronald E. Nocks, Teacher, Professional Actor

"Betty Meabon—a most remarkable woman—not only is she a retired registered nurse and world traveler, but as a gifted musician she has taught music for almost fifty years. Aside from those notable accomplishments, she is a devoted wife of more than 54 years, a mother, grandmother, and great grandmother. From her rich varied background she shares her love for life and offers her keen insight in *Step by Step: A Collection of Poems of Inspiration and Travel.* Those who partake of her poetry will be strengthened and encouraged by selections in "Inspirational Thoughts and Blessings" Her poems touch the heart and minister to readers in a gentle reassuring way. She shares her appreciation for the changing 'Seasons of Life' and displays the deep love she has for her family. Her poetry is also a vehicle through which she expresses her devotion to her Lord and to her church where a number of poems were written to commemorate specific occasions of celebration. Having traveled extensively in the Americas and abroad, Betty takes her readers on an informative and most engaging trek to see 'People and Places beyond the Familiar.' For Betty Meabon, indeed, 'Life is a journey. . .,' and she invites you to join her, as she shares from her heart and soul while Enjoying the Journey. . . along life's highway."

Lonnell E. Johnson, Ph.D.
Professor Emeritus
Otterbein College

"For many years Betty Meabon has written poetry for family and friends as a way to commemorate their special occasions or celebrate events in their lives. Mostly, though, she has used poetry to chronicle her life's journey, both spiritual and actual, and the insights she has gained along the way.

Lucky for us, Betty shares her faith and wisdom in *Step by Step*. This wonderful anthology celebrates her devotion to family and friends, her appreciation of the grand and the commonplace in everyday life, her love of nature, and the richness of the human experience.

Whether writing about her world travels or reflecting on the everyday joys and challenges of life, Betty's poems inform, inspire, and encourage readers with humor and grace. They prompt us to seize moments during our busy days to ponder life's mysteries and wonders. They encourage us to practice the fine art of "stick-to-itiveness" and persevere when faced with a challenge. They also remind us to appreciate what we have and value our unique talents so that we may live fully and generously.

Readers will savor Betty's poems not only for their power to delight and inspire but also for their rich sounds and rhythms. They will find themselves returning again and again to *Step by Step* and treasure its place in their library."

Ann Ullom-Morse
Attorney at Law